TANKS
IN CAMERA

TANKS
IN CAMERA

ARCHIVE PHOTOGRAPHS FROM THE TANK MUSEUM

THE WESTERN DESERT
1940–1943

DAVID FLETCHER

Budding
BOOKS

A Budding Book

This edition published in 2000 by Budding Books,
an imprint of Sutton Publishing Limited
Phoenix Mill · Thrupp · Stroud · Gloucestershire GL5 2BU

First published in 1998 by Sutton Publishing Limited

A catalogue record for this book is available from the British Library

ISBN 1 84015 110 2

Typeset in 11/15pt Baskerville.
Typesetting and origination by
Sutton Publishing Limted.
Printed in Great Britain by
Redwood Books,
Trowbridge, Wiltshire.

CONTENTS

NOTE ON PHOTOGRAPHS

Many of the photographs presented in this book were taken under varying, often difficult conditions and rarely by a professional photographer. They are included in this collection for their value as historical documents rather than for their photographic quality.

INTRODUCTION

The great North African desert which we are taught at school to call the Sahara covers some 3,500,000 square miles. It is a geographical entity but not a political one since it is crossed by the invisible frontiers of many countries of which just three concern us here. From the east they are Egypt, Libya and Tunisia – Libya itself was subdivided historically into Cyrenaica and Tripolitania. This area represents about a quarter of the whole Sahara, if that, but in human terms it is still vast and dramatically inhospitable. Even so a select few survive there. Some are born to it, others take to it – the rest have to cope as best they can.

As a battleground it would appear to have little to commend it since there is nothing obvious to fight over. Yet there are those who would claim that it is ideal. Few non-combatants are likely to suffer and where there is no settled population there will be no cities or farms to knock about. Unable to live off the land, armies are fighting the environment as much as they are one another and when European troops have found themselves in such alien territory it has tended to emphasize their common humanity.

This is probably one reason why the battles fought there between 1940 and 1943 continue to exercise such fascination, which, in turn, is the excuse for this book. It is by no means the first, nor will it be the last, but it has been compiled with the purpose of illustrating armoured warfare in the region as far as possible through the medium of soldiers' snapshots. Over the years the library of the Tank Museum at Bovington in Dorset has acquired a huge collection of photographs taken by serving soldiers. Strictly speaking private photography was illegal but many soldiers on both sides ignored the rule. And it is well that they did. It not only means that we are left with a larger collection of prints than might otherwise be the case, we also get to see those things that attracted the soldiers' attention, which is not always the same thing that attracted the official war photographers'. They might not be perfect examples of the photographer's art but they are very much the genuine article and well worth studying. Official photographs are used to illustrate significant aspects of the story when nothing else is available, and this is most evident in the chapters dealing with the fighting in Tunisia.

Wherever possible, photographs, even some of poor quality, have been selected because they illustrate precisely the events being described. However there are instances where, in the absence of something specific, the author has chosen the next best thing.

The format will become obvious from a quick scan. Eight chapters cover significant stages in the desert war, each with a general introduction leading up to a photographic section with extended captions to provide the atmosphere and detail of the time. Tanks dominate, naturally, but other armoured vehicles are included and it does not end there; transport, landscapes and incidents in the tank soldier's life are recorded as well.

Those who detect a strong British bias will not be mistaken. It is unavoidable. Virtually every album or photograph donated was supplied by a British soldier who tended to focus on his own unit. If he saw a German or Italian tank in a situation where he could take a snap of it then it was inevitably knocked out or captured. However, in order to give the subject a wide coverage and do justice to all concerned, the collection has been examined in great detail to produce views of both Allied and enemy equipment.

Even to those with a casual interest in the subject names like Tobruk or El Alamein will be familiar, but in three years of almost continual warfare many other names appeared in the headlines. Most describe natural features or vestiges of human settlement while some appear to have been just names on a map with nothing showing on the ground. If a name was needed where none existed then it had to be created and in most instances invention lost out to familiarity which is why one finds another Knightsbridge and King's Cross, among others, in unlikely settings.

The sand, they say, is never still although it is largely undisturbed. Track marks left by passing vehicles have been known to remain visible for years on the desert surface. There must have been occasions during the Second World War when vehicles operating well away from the normal routes came across evidence of vehicles from the First World War, or from the years between. Did they wonder how they got there? Did they even realize that armoured vehicles had been operating in the region since 1915? Before we come to 1940, and the years that followed, perhaps it would help to form some sort of picture of those earlier times.

The first British armoured cars to arrive in the desert were Rolls-Royces of Nos 3 and 4 Squadrons, Royal Naval Air Service which had not been landed on the Gallipoli beachhead. Established as the Emergency Squadron and based at Alexandria in June 1915 they were given the task of patrolling the Egyptian frontier. The section of three shown here has been halted in such a way that their guns cover the surrounding area.

Three Armoured Motor Batteries, equipped with Rolls-Royce armoured cars and commanded by Major the Duke of Westminster, arrived in Egypt in January 1916. A month later they were shipped west, to Mersah Matruh and from there moved further west to Sollum. From here, in March, the Duke set out with his armoured cars supported by Ford T pick-up trucks on a 200-mile round trip to rescue the crew of the steamer *Tara*, held prisoner at Bir Hacheim.

The Model T Fords proved so successful in the desert that from March 1916 they were formed into Light Car Patrols which operated independently of the Rolls-Royces. In February 1917 a combined force of armoured cars and Fords captured the enemy base at Siwa oasis, deep in the desert, and the garrison posted there was supplied continually by Ford convoys. These Fords, all stripped to the bare essentials, were photographed at an oasis. Most of them are shielded from the sun.

In April 1916 the Australians contributed an armoured car section of their own, comprising Daimler and Mercedes armoured cars, a Minerva pick-up truck – or tender – and a crude motorcycle machine-gun combination. They served with 11 and 12 Light Armoured Car Batteries as part of the Western Frontier Force for a while but, proving unsuitable for desert operations, were shipped back to Australia in 1917.

In order to maintain law and order in Cairo the British military authorities ordered the construction of an enormous armoured lorry, based on a chain-drive Commer chassis and known as *Mother*. Fully armoured, even to the wheel hubs, it mounted two turrets, each with a Maxim machine-gun, and had loopholes in the sides for the crew to use rifles, as demonstrated here. Detachable planks on each side could be used to get across ditches or patches of soft sand and they were evidently used, as the tyre marks show.

In June 1920 the newly constituted No. 3 Armoured Car Company, now an element of the Tank Corps, arrived in Egypt to undertake internal security duties. In 1921 serious rioting broke out. Three Italian sailors were murdered by the mob in Alexandria and a section of armoured cars was sent down there to restore order. Two of the cars, wartime pattern Rolls-Royces, are seen here at their headquarters in the city.

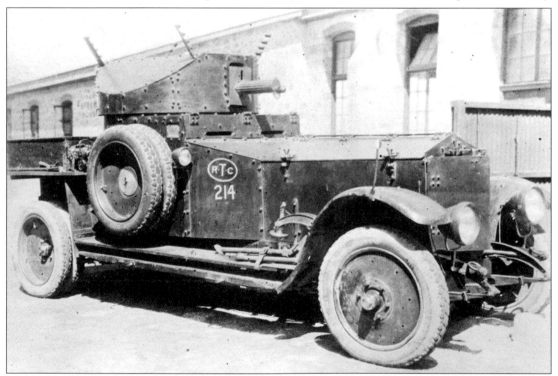

The 3rd Armoured Car Company – Royal Tank Corps from 1923 – soon found that the wartime armoured cars were wearing out. Until new ones became available new chassis were sent out from Britain onto which the old bodies were transferred. This example is equipped with a wireless and the tripod for a dismounted machine-gun is on the running board. Notice in addition the extra spare wheels. The desert punished pneumatic tyres severely.

The British fascination with the desert affected a group of young officers based in Cairo, and one in particular, Ralph Bagnold of the Royal Signals, organized desert expeditions during leave periods. Starting with a Ford T, which he later exchanged for the Model A shown here, Bagnold led a series of trips into the Libyan and Sinai deserts between 1925 and 1932. His book *Libyan Sands*, first published in 1935, proved an inspiration to wartime desert soldiers.

The first section of tanks to arrive in Egypt were the so-called Vickers Mediums from 3rd Battalion Royal Tank Corps in Britain. Fitted with Armstrong-Siddeley air-cooled V8 engines, they had been designed with hot climates in mind but they were temperamental machines at the best of times and, since no transporters were available, they never ventured far into the desert. This unusual view shows the underside of a Medium, as it is lifted out of the hold of a ship at Alexandria.

Royal Tank Corps strength in the region was increased in 1929 when 5th Armoured Car Company was posted there after nearly two years in Shanghai. This Rolls-Royce, displaying the commander's hood and front bumper acquired in Shanghai, arrived with the 5th, was later used by 12th Royal Lancers and is shown here in a silver and black camouflage serving with 11th Hussars. This car later came back to Britain and is now on show at the Tank Museum.

The mechanization of the British cavalry dates from 1928 when both 11th Hussars and 12th Lancers exchanged their horses for armoured cars. The latter were already in Egypt and took over Rolls-Royces from 3rd Armoured Car Company. New cars arrived later and here a crew struggles to release their car from some very soft sand. This is one of the later 1924 Pattern cars which had improved hull and turret design.

By 1933 it had been decided to create a new Royal Tank Corps tank battalion in Egypt. It was achieved by amalgamating the two Royal Tank Corps armoured car companies to form the 6th Battalion which, for a while, ran a mixed force of tanks and armoured cars. Here two 1924 Pattern Rolls-Royces form the supports for a hoist while the engine is lifted out of a Medium Tank. Note the dark colour of the cars compared with the light shade of the tank.

The 11th Hussars replaced the 12th Lancers in 1934. It was a time of heightened tension when Mussolini ordered Italian troops to invade Abyssinia and these two 1920 Pattern Rolls-Royces are seen behind sandbagged emplacements near the Libyan frontier. The contraption on the turret of the nearer car is an improvised seat from which the commanding officer could scan the desert when the regiment was patrolling.

Interest in the performance of vehicles in the desert increased and by 1934 a branch of the Mechanisation Experimental Establishment (Farnborough) was functioning in Egypt. These two huge Lanchester six-wheeled armoured cars were shipped out for tests by MEE and the user regiments but they proved too heavy for desert service. The car already on the dockside is a Mark II with a Mark I still in slings. The colour scheme is said to have been sand, overpainted with patches of dark red.

As confidence grew more long-range desert excursions were mounted. They had the advantages of testing machines and providing navigational and survival skills for the men. This untidy group appears to be a lunchtime break in the middle of nowhere. On the left a Morris-Commercial 30-cwt six-wheeler with a Guy or Leyland 3-tonner wireless lorry alongside. The car (extreme right) is a Riley and the party in the foreground looks like the officers' mess in full swing. Some of these trips covered vast distances down the Nile valley and well out into the desert.

Similar excursions with tanks generally stayed nearer to Cairo but they also helped to hone desert skills. This Medium tank of 6th Battalion, towing a water trailer, is crossing the railway using spare sleepers to prevent damage to the rails. The tank is a Mark IIA, one of the few sent out to Egypt with the hull clad in panels of asbestos in an effort to reduce the heat inside. The experiment does not appear to have had the desired effect.

A very unusual sight in the desert, and not just for the variety of headgear. This is the band of the 11th Hussars on a desert outing. Most seem to be wearing full European uniform despite the heat, and what appears to be a kettle drum is lying, skin down, on the top of the lorry. This looks like a tea break so presumably they were in the desert on business, playing for the troops.

New, three-man light tanks were appearing in Britain from about 1935 and this Light Mark VI was the first one taken to Egypt for desert trials. It must have done extremely well because it is seen here against the remarkable architecture of Siwa oasis, deep in the Egyptian desert. One local is clearly fascinated by the cameraman but nobody is paying very much attention to the tank.

When the threat from Italy was at its greatest a Mobile Force was created, including tanks, armoured cars, artillery and motorized infantry. It was disbanded in August 1936 but reactivated in a slightly different form under General P.C.S. Hobart who initiated a period of intensive training in September 1938. This was the force which would later become 7th Armoured Division, the famous Desert Rats. Whether Hobart would have approved of this First World War-style attack by infantry and Vickers Mediums of 6th Battalion is doubtful.

By 1938 there were two light tank units in Egypt: 7th Hussars and 1st Battalion Royal Tank Corps. Light Tanks Mark VIA of the latter are shown here parading through Cairo. On the left is a Morris-Commercial CS9 Light Armoured Car of 11th Hussars which on this occasion is acting as the saluting base for Lieutenant-General H.M. (Jumbo) Wilson, GOC British Forces in Egypt. Wilson was instrumental in sacking Hobart from his command.

Preparing for war. Mark VIA Light Tanks on outpost duty in the desert. They belong to C Squadron, 1st Battalion Royal Tank Corps. The Lewis gun, mounted on the commander's cupola, is an uncommon feature but it will be noted that by now virtually all tanks were fitted with wireless. On either side of the turret are mounted 4-in smoke dischargers and the sand guards, covering the front section of the tracks, are a feature seen only in the Middle East.

CHAPTER 1
THE RACE TO BEDA FOMM

Once war was declared in Europe it seemed only a matter of time before it spread to the Middle East. The Italians had substantial forces in Libya to threaten Egypt and more in Ethiopia, Eritrea and Italian Somaliland posing a threat to British forces in the Sudan and Kenya. They were, however, checkmated to some extent by the French presence in Algeria and Tunisia and their declaration of war, on 10 June 1940, seems to have been calculated to reduce that risk as far as possible. Quite what they expected from the relatively small British force is unclear but what they got was a surprise.

The Italians had marked the frontier between Libya and Egypt by an impressive barbed wire and stake fence, backed by a dispersed chain of forts which were supplied from the fortified ports of Bardia and Tobruk. Within twenty-four hours of the declaration of war armoured cars of the 11th Hussars were creating gaps in the wire, using a technique developed during trials on a replica length of fence at Mersah Matruh, and passing through to harass the enemy positions. In practice this meant spending each night on the Libyan side of the wire, trying to estimate the strength of the forts which covered the frontier and beating up any transport moving between them.

Considering that these attacks were being carried out by one regiment in thinly armoured cars that did not even have four-wheel drive it is remarkable that within a week the Italians were evacuating their forts, and when 11th Hussars were joined by the 7th Hussars, with their tanks, the significant Fort Capuzzo was taken. British confidence was running high, encouraging the troops to take risks, leading to incidents in which single armoured cars attacked Italian light tanks with every expectation of victory. Success was not inevitable and the Italian artillery, in particular, fought it out to the last. However, the Italian field commander, Marshal Rodolfo Graziani, entrusted the immediate defence of the frontier to his air force and started to gather his ground troops for a major attack on Egypt. At the same time his British counterpart, General Sir Archibald Wavell, was becoming concerned about the state of his tanks. Continuous operations, however successful, rapidly reduced their reliability and more than one operation was jeopardized when tanks broke down during an approach march.

The 8th Hussars moved up to the frontier in mid-July; like the 7th Hussars they were part of 4th Armoured Brigade. General Hobart's erstwhile Mobile Division had now become 7th Armoured Division, part of the Western Desert Force. The division's organization was dictated in part by pre-war concepts in that it had a light armoured brigade (the 4th) and a heavy (the 7th) along with what was known as the Support Group. Thus, besides the divisional armoured car regiment – the 11th Hussars with their Rolls-Royce and Morris vehicles – the two Hussar regiments had light tanks while the two Royal Tank Regiments (1st and 6th) had cruisers. This, at least, was the theory. In practice the light tank regiments were reinforced by a smattering of cruisers while the heavy regiments, which were short of cruisers anyway, had their numbers made up by light tanks. Even this must be qualified by the fact that the limited reliability of British tanks, especially the cruisers, usually meant that about one third were in for repair at any given time. The divisional support group consisted of a battery of 25-pdr guns and two motorized rifle battalions.

Italian armour was certainly no better, and there was less of it. Their armoured cars were more than a match for the British models but their light tanks, the ubiquitous CV3/33 tankettes, were little more than armoured death traps. The main medium tank, the type M11/39, was hampered by the location of its principal gun in the hull, alongside the driver, but the more modern M13/40 was a perfectly respectable machine by contemporary standards. The Italian Army also made considerable use of lorry-mounted artillery of various types. Nevertheless Graziani's armour suffered just as much from reliability problems and it was rarely employed with the dash necessary to achieve striking results. The British soon came to the conclusion that the Italians did not like surprises.

This became even more evident in September when Graziani made his anticipated move eastwards. It was revealed not just by the increasingly bold activity noted by patrols of the 11th Hussars but also by the fact that his offensive was broadcast to the Italian people from Rome. The British made no attempt to hold any of the frontier posts they had taken but retired ahead of the advancing Italians to the prepared defences at Mersah Matruh. Long troop convoys brought the Italians forward, screened by their armour to the south since rumours were rife of a massive British tank force, deep in the desert, which was awaiting its chance to strike. Caution was the watchword every kilometre of the way; all potential points of resistance were subjected to a heavy artillery barrage and formal attack but in fact there was no resistance, except from the air, and that was fairly evenly matched. Having moved some 60 miles in four days the Italians were at least in Egypt, but still a good 60 miles from the British position at Mersah Matruh, when they halted by the coastal settlement of Sidi Barrani and settled down. From here a small force was pushed forward to Makita, further along the coast, while the main force spread out south and west, establishing posts as it went at Nibeiwa on the coastal plain and a cluster around Sofafi and Rabia on the edge of the desert escarpment. Over the next three months these camps were developed into strong fortified zones but they suffered from the defect that they were too far apart to provide mutual support in the event of attack. Despite pressure from Rome Graziani refused to move again until his deficit in armour was made good and the manpower of his force increased. Meanwhile, bored with their defensive posture, British units, nicknamed 'Jock Columns', again started patrolling and raiding, having discovered that it was a simple matter to pass between the Italian strongpoints and operate in their rear.

Towards the end of September three more armoured regiments arrived from Britain, having sailed the long route around the Cape rather than risk the Mediterranean. These were the 3rd Hussars, which had been slightly involved in the Norwegian campaign, 2nd Royal Tank Regiment (RTR), which had fought with 1st Armoured Division in France, and 7th RTR, which had formed part of 1st Army Tank Brigade in the same campaign. The 3rd Hussars and 2nd RTR were destined to join 7th Armoured Division – the former with light tanks, the latter with cruisers – while 7th RTR was the first genuine infantry tank battalion to arrive in the theatre. It was equipped with A12 Matilda infantry tanks, the first such machines to be seen in the desert. However they were not seen yet. Wavell appreciated their power and wished to keep them under

wraps for the present. He was beginning to realize that a further Italian move was unlikely in the immediate future and had every intention of seizing the initiative.

While two of the new regiments moved out to join the division and acquire a feel for the desert, 7th RTR went into a period of intensive training with 4th Indian Division for what would become known as Operation Compass. As conceived by Wavell and controlled by Major-General Richard O'Connor Compass was to be a massive raid on the Italian position north of the escarpment with the object of driving the Italians out of Egypt. The plan was to send the two armoured brigades through the 20-mile gap south of the Italian fortified camp at Nibeiwa and have them swing north to block the coast road. Meanwhile 7th RTR and the Indians would make a tighter turn and move against the Italian posts from the rear, taking them out one at a time until they reached the coastal camp at Sidi Barrani.

The attack on Nibeiwa began on the morning of 10 December 1940 and it was immediately successful. Indeed it went so well that Lieutenant-Colonel R.M. Jerram, commanding 7th RTR, went on to capture three more posts in the afternoon and Sidi Barrani itself the next day, although by then he was down to just eight running tanks. The southern posts around Rabia and Sofafi were simply abandoned by the Italians without a fight. Vast numbers of prisoners were taken but more got away, heading west for the Libyan frontier. The attempt by 7th Armoured Brigade to cut them off was delayed and by the time 3rd Hussars caught up the Italians had created an effective defensive position at Buq-Buq, close to the coast. In attempting to attack, the regiment's light tanks ran into a salt marsh where they became bogged down and were subsequently blown apart by enemy gunfire. The situation was saved by the 8th Hussars and a squadron of cruisers from 2nd RTR. Two days later, on 14 December, 3rd Hussars were across the frontier accepting the surrender of Fort Capuzzo and Operation Compass had already exceeded all expectations.

With his army evicted from Egypt Mussolini directed that it should make a stand at the well-defended port of Bardia. Having spent Christmas in the desert the Western Desert Force learned that it was to be renamed XIIIth Corps on 1 January 1941 and that 4th Indian Division would be replaced by 6th Australian Division, newly arrived from Palestine. The Australians, well aware of the reputation of the Matildas, cooperated to the full and within three days Bardia was in Allied hands. The amount of material captured was staggering but the number of prisoners now outnumbered the entire British garrison in Egypt. Investing in success, Wavell now permitted O'Connor to tackle Tobruk, 70 miles to the west, but by this stage the armoured element of his force was nearly worn out. The 7th RTR was down to eighteen Matildas while, in 7th Armoured Division, 8th Hussars and 6th RTR handed their surviving tanks over to the other regiments and went back to Cairo.

The assault on Tobruk began on 21 January and was virtually complete by the end of the following day. While the Matildas and Australian infantry systematically worked their way to the dock area the more mobile tanks of 7th Armoured Division kept the approaches free from the threat of counter-attack. Once again vast numbers of prisoners were taken but the main Italian Army began a lengthy, fighting retreat along the coast road through Derna and Barce to Benghazi. There was a much quicker route, a direct, straight line from Tobruk to Agedabia on the Gulf of Sidra but it was difficult ground and quite unsuitable for an army that was not fully mechanized and incapable of carrying sufficient water with it. Even so the coastal route was no easy option for either side and the Italians were by no means ready to give up. They made a strong stand at Derna but, once the Australians had driven them out by 29 January, O'Connor decided upon a gamble.

His plan was to release as much of 7th Armoured Division as he could spare along the shorter inland route with a view to cutting off the Italian retreat at a location known as Beda Fomm, north of Agedabia. The expedition started out on 4 February but it proved hard going for the tanks. In an effort to get some sort of road block in place the armoured cars of 11th Hussars with a newly arrived squadron from the King's Dragoon Guards, along with a motorized infantry battalion, a battery of 25-pdrs and nine anti-tank guns carried on lorries, took the lead. Commanded by Colonel J.F.B. Combe and known as Combeforce it was in position the next day and not a moment too soon. The Australians were at the gates of Benghazi, which fell on 6 February, and an 11-mile long column of Italian infantry was approaching the road block.

It did not prove difficult to halt the column. It had no tanks or artillery support and, despite desperate attempts to break through, it was trapped. Even so the pressure was building up from behind and there was only so much a small force could do; it was all a matter of whether the tanks could get there on time. By late afternoon 4th Armoured Brigade, consisting of 3rd Hussars, 7th Hussars and 2nd RTR, was beginning to arrive. As each regiment appeared it was directed to a point overlooking the road on the west side from which it proceeded to wreak havoc upon the jumble of enemy troops and vehicles. Night gave the Italians some respite and by the next day their artillery and some sixty M13/40 Medium tanks had arrived. These were now organized to make a more concerted attack which at times looked like succeeding but when 1st RTR, the last surviving regiment from 7th Armoured Brigade, arrived the Italians began to realize the futility of their position. After a last, fierce attack on Combeforce early on 7 February those who had not managed to get away surrendered and the British victory in North Africa was complete.

That this should be the ultimate result of a raid is surprising enough but the implications were even greater. British and Commonwealth troops now effectively controlled the southern and eastern shores of the Mediterranean with all that implied for the exercise of naval and air power. If the Greek and Albanian armies proved capable of withstanding Italian attacks

then Italy might be virtually out of the war and Britain would be able to concentrate on Germany in the north. The lesson was not lost upon the Spanish dictator, General Franco, who promptly decided not to join the Axis, but it also rang alarm bells in Berlin. Hitler also understood the situation and, probably against his better judgment, agreed to provide troops to bolster Mussolini's remaining forces in Libya. At least twice already in the campaign British forces had spotted German aircraft passing overhead but the full meaning of this potential threat was not appreciated.

In any case the forces that finally defeated the Italians at Beda Fomm were worn out and had to be withdrawn to Egypt. Yet beyond Beda Fomm, Tripoli beckoned and with it total control of the Italian colony. The 11th Hussars probed as far west as El Agheila, on the border between Cyrenaica and Tripolitania where they captured the fort, but they got no further. O'Connor was convinced, tired as they were, that his men could capitalize on their success and wrap up the entire country and Wavell might have supported him, had he not been under extreme pressure from London. Being, perhaps, better aware of the larger picture the Prime Minister ordered Wavell to switch his main effort to Greece, where a German attack looked like succeeding, and there was no option but to obey. The short campaign in Greece was a disaster, although it delayed Hitler's planned attack on the Soviet Union for a few significant weeks, but the repercussions for North Africa were unfortunate, to say the least.

The Italian frontier wire, 5 ft high and 400 miles long. It was described by the British at the time as being rusty and it did not prove much of an obstacle, even to armoured cars. The 11th Hussars developed a technique which involved crushing it flat with a Rolls-Royce and then nudging the upright pickets until they snapped.

A Rolls-Royce of 11th Hussars at speed. This version, fitted with wider wheels and large section sand tyres, first appeared in 1924. Early in the war they were modified by removing the original turret and fitting a light, open-top version which mounted (from the left) a Boys anti-tank rifle, Bren light machine-gun and smoke-bomb discharger. Notice also the water condensing can by the offside front wheel.

An Italian CV3/33 tankette lying, damaged, in the desert. It carried a crew of two and was normally armed with a pair of medium machine-guns. Armour at the front was 13.5 mm thick, 8.5 mm at the sides but only 6 mm elsewhere. It was powered by a Fiat four-cylinder petrol engine. The lack of a turret was its biggest handicap. In order to hit anything the driver virtually had to aim the entire tank.

British light tanks on patrol. This is the Mark VIB, which had 16-mm armour, a crew of three and two machine-guns, one heavy and one medium. Powered by a Meadows six-cylinder engine it had a good top speed and, of course, with a rotating turret it was far more flexible in action. Note that even these light British tanks all had radio. The Italians were not so lucky in this respect and it limited their flexibility in action.

Although much criticized later there was not much wrong with the British cruiser tanks of 1940. This is the type A10, or Cruiser Mark II, armed with a 40-mm gun and protected by 30 mm of armour. It is powered by an AEC petrol engine and has a range, on good ground, of about 100 miles. Accuracy of the gun depended to a considerable extent upon the skill of the gunner who controlled the weapon's elevation with his shoulder – not easy in a fast-moving tank on rough ground.

An Italian armoured car or *Autoblinda*. This SPA-Ansaldo-built AB41 was a much better machine than anything the 11th Hussars possessed. It was armed with a 20-mm cannon, had four-wheel drive and was very fast. Unfortunately the Italians did not exploit the cavalry tradition with armoured cars and tended to use them for limited reconnaissance and convoy escort duties.

An M11/39 Medium tank at speed. The main, 47-mm weapon is in the hull, which restricts its field of fire, while the turret contains only machine-guns. In hot weather, when not in action, two of the crew elect to travel outside, leaving the driver to suffer the unpleasant conditions of the interior alone. Mechanically most Italian vehicles were well designed, in the tradition of their motor industry, but as fighting machines they left a great deal to be desired.

The Italians mounted everything from light anti-tank guns to heavy anti-aircraft guns on lorries to improve mobility over the desert. In this case a battery of 105-mm howitzers is posed for the camera. The carrying vehicle is the Lancia 3RO heavy lorry, a conventional type powered by a five-cylinder diesel engine.

The Matilda was a tank designed for European conditions which made quite a name for itself in the desert. It carried the same 40-mm gun as contemporary British cruisers but it was protected by frontal armour nearly 80 mm thick. Although powered by a pair of six-cylinder diesel engines it was a very slow tank since it was designed to work with the infantry. This one, newly arrived in Egypt with 7th RTR, is carried on a transporter trailer.

The 4th Indian Division, commanded by General Noel Beresford-Pierce, consisted of two Indian brigades and one British. It always enjoyed an excellent reputation and its performance against the Italian positions in the Egyptian desert speaks for itself. In this photograph, clearly contrived for official release, a line of men in open order advances behind a Bren Gun Carrier. These versatile machines, powered by a Ford V8 engine, could be found wherever British or Commonwealth troops were serving.

The attack on Sidi Barrani. With an artillery barrage evident on the horizon a troop of three Matildas from 7th RTR moves in to attack the Italian positions. Colonel Jerram took immense care of his precious regiment. He always allowed more than enough time for each move, so that the tanks travelled slowly and did not break down. He also insisted that as soon as they had completed their tasks in an attack the tanks should regroup at once for further orders; he was thus able to conserve his regiment's strength.

Italian prisoners were rounded up in such numbers that they were often left to make their own way into captivity. The first staging post in their journey back to Egypt was Mersah Matruh where large areas were fenced off to contain them. Guards were hardly necessary, there being nowhere to go, but in this view at least an old Medium tank of 6th RTR has been pressed into service just in case.

Although Allied casualties were ridiculously light when compared with those suffered by the Italians, there was still a price to be paid. Here wounded, probably from 4th Indian Division, wait to be evacuated from a regimental aid post, no more than a patch of desert scrub, by Chevrolet light ambulances.

Overlooked by the dunes at Buq-Buq, where the Italians established a strong defensive position, light tanks of 3rd Hussars lie wrecked and abandoned in the salt flats which claimed so many of them. This unfortunate situation, which marred an otherwise almost perfect action, resulted in the main simply from a lack of experience in desert operations. Often such experience can only be gained the hard way.

A Cruiser Mark IV of A Squadron, 2nd RTR. Tanks of this type employed the American Christie suspension which enabled them to travel at speed over very rough ground. In this case the top speed could be as much as 30 mph. Notice how the radio aerial could be folded back to reduce its prominence although in this case the commander has left his turret machine-gun sticking up in the air. The striped object on the side of the turret was used for silent signalling from tank to tank.

The artillery barrage that preceded the assault on Bardia was the greatest yet delivered during the North African campaign. Even viewed from this very safe distance it is clear that the enemy positions are taking a constant and thorough pounding. Continual pressure from the small British force sapped Italian morale but it was not helped by bombastic signals from Mussolini, safe in Rome, urging his men to die bravely rather than retreat.

Constant movement and fighting nearly every day took a heavy toll of British tanks, even of Jerram's carefully husbanded Matildas. In this view the nearest tank is having some suspension units replaced, possibly as a result of mine damage. A shelter has been erected alongside and much of the work is probably being done by the crew. Quite often tanks left behind in the morning would come trundling up later in the day, eager to rejoin the fray, but only after crew members and unit fitters had worked like fury to repair them.

For some time during this period, the 11th Hussars had an extra D Squadron which was in fact created from No. 2 Armoured Car Company, RAF, brought in from Palestine. Although their cars started life as Rolls-Royces, and still looked much the same, the armoured bodies had been transferred onto Fordson chassis. Since they probably appreciated the threat from air attack more than most, the RAF boys liked to have an extra pair of light machine-guns on top of the turret.

The crew of a Bren Carrier watches as infantry advance on an enemy position. For all the thunder of the artillery or the majesty of a charge by heavy tanks it was normally here that the real work was done. Men on foot, armed with rifles and protected by steel helmets, covered every inch of the ground, dealing with the enemy man to man. Tanks might achieve an initial advantage but only these men could occupy the positions they had taken and remain ready to deal with a counter-attack. This was the unchanging face of war.

British troops knew two kinds of Italian mine which they nicknamed according to their shape. The anti-tank version was called the 'coffin' mine, its anti-personnel counterpart being the 'thermos' mine. Even this could break the track of a tank. In this case the victim is a Cruiser Mark I, or A9, identified by the two auxiliary machine-gun turrets at the front. They were nothing but a nuisance, being far too cramped and stuffy for desert conditions.

Cruisers of 2nd RTR during an advance to action. Notice how the column is well spread out to minimize the risk from air attack. The broken nature of the ground is clear – tough on the tank and demanding constant attention from the driver. At Beda Fomm, even after a long and difficult drive, these tanks were committed to action as soon as they arrived on the scene and continued fighting while there was still light enough to see.

The road from Benghazi, looking north, in the aftermath of Beda Fomm. A Morris truck and armoured car of B Squadron King's Dragoon Guards weave their way through abandoned Italian vehicles. Note how their artillery has been wheeled out to face east, the direction from which the British tanks attacked, in a desperate effort to shield their comrades.

A cluster of Italian M13/40 Medium tanks abandoned after their last fight at Beda Fomm. The gun is 47 mm, the armour a respectable 30 mm but the speed a rather desperate 19 mph despite being powered by an excellent Fiat V8 engine. The large side door was no doubt a blessing in the desert and an ideal means of escape in an emergency but it created a serious weakness in the structure of the tank. Many British tanks were of riveted construction but the Italians had some plates bolted in place and this could be a lethal arrangement if it was hit.

There are more British vehicles in this scene than Italian types. This picture was taken some time after the battle when everything worth having had been taken away and the wrecks dragged clear of the road. The M13/40 tank in the foreground has suffered grievously. A massive internal explosion has removed the turret and side door, gutted the interior and dislodged many of the front hull plates.

CHAPTER 2
ROMMEL ARRIVES

Although Hitler believed that Germany had no interest in North Africa his naval advisers saw things differently. If the British were left to dominate the eastern Mediterranean and the Suez Canal it could have a serious effect on Axis communications. In October 1940 General Ritter von Thoma had visited the area but it was at a time when the Italians appeared to have everything under control and they seemed to be more interested in German equipment than troops. When Bardia fell Hitler authorized air attacks against British shipping in the area and he was already making plans to send troops. However, there would be conditions.

General Rommel learned that he would command German forces in Libya early in February 1941 and he flew out there almost at once. Hitler's view was that the German forces would be there to act in a defensive role, to prevent the British from taking Tripoli. Later he altered this view to the extent that a Panzer division might be included to undertake a more active defence but this was all on the understanding that German forces were not to be exposed to risk of losses, either in equipment or personnel. In such circumstances the selection of Rommel as commander might seem to be less than prudent.

For the British, frustrated at not being allowed to finish the job by taking Tripoli, a relatively passive role was equally welcome. What was left of 7th Armoured Division had been pulled back to Egypt to refit, the idea being to replace it with 2nd Armoured Division which had just arrived from Britain in a rather sorry state. Its 1st Armoured Brigade was required at once for Churchill's intervention in Greece and all that was left of 3rd Armoured Brigade was 5th RTR. This, along with the divisional armoured car regiment, the King's Dragoon Guards, was sent west to join 3rd Hussars and 6th RTR at Agedabia. These two regiments were now equipped with the remaining light tanks and all the serviceable M13/40s that had been captured at Beda Fomm. All of the equipment was in a dreadful state. The 5th RTR's cruisers were hardly in good shape when they arrived in Egypt and the long run west had virtually finished them off.

The light tanks were all on their last legs, while the Italian machines were too slow to be of much use and, apart from their effective guns, could not be relied upon.

Not that the Germans were in a much better state. Their 5th Light Division had two under-strength battalions and about one third of the tanks were Panzers I and II, armed only with machine-guns. Rommel increased his apparent strength by creating dummy tanks on *Kubelwagen* chassis and, with the advantage of local air superiority, began to practise his policy of active defence. He launched a probing attack at the end of March which triggered a British withdrawal that swiftly got out of hand. Like O'Connor, Rommel followed the coastal route to maintain pressure on the British and Australian forces while using the shorter, but more difficult, inland route to try to cut them off. This created such confusion that the orderly British withdrawal turned into a complete rout. Misunderstandings, compounded by mistakes, cost the Allies dear but the Germans gained valuable desert experience very quickly while Rommel himself acquired a reputation that virtually hypnotized his opponents.

On the British side things were chaotic. On more than one occasion friendly forces retreating were mistaken for enemy troops advancing and valuable dumps of fuel and ammunition were destroyed prematurely. Three senior British officers were captured and on at least one occasion a complete artillery regiment vanished. Where regiments kept their heads they inflicted delays on the Germans but invariably they were then given conflicting orders and found themselves at a disadvantage. If not they would ultimately run out of fuel and have to abandon their tanks. Amid all this chaos one small British unit might be singled out as an exception. The Long Range Desert Group, operating in modified Chevrolet trucks, was something of a law unto itself but it was a thorn in the flesh of the Afrika Korps. Major Ralph Bagnold, who was mentioned in the Introduction, was one of its founders but it soon attracted a group of freebooting volunteers from the British and New Zealand armies, who learned to live, navigate, fight and survive on trips that carried them deep into the desert. The Group specialized in sabotage and intelligence gathering although, as things became more formalized, it tended to relinquish the former role to the Special Air Service.

The 15th Panzer Division reached Tripoli in late April/early May and was soon in action. It is instructive to compare the speed with which newly arrived Panzer units were hurried to the front with the relatively leisurely process followed by the British. The Germans, of course, only had to face a short sea route while the British were at sea for weeks, coming all the way around Africa via the Cape to avoid the risks of running through the Mediterranean. Even so, once they arrived in Egypt the tanks had to spend a good deal of time in workshops being prepared for the desert while the men were given time to acclimatize. The Germans enjoyed no such luxury. Yet their tanks were no more designed for desert conditions than the British types. Indeed at one time the Germans were experiencing endless breakdowns caused, it was claimed, by a type of oil filter unsuitable for desert conditions. The difference seems to have been that the Germans were prepared to react much more swiftly to these problems than were the British.

Tobruk held out, despite repeated attempts to take it, but the Germans cleared the British out of every other location in Libya. The key position, as far as both sides were concerned, was Halfaya Pass near Sollum where the coast road climbs onto the main desert plateau. Wavell's Operation Brevity, launched in May, was an attempt to catch the German and Italian forces off guard using the surviving British tanks and Matildas of the newly arrived 4th RTR.

Initially successful the attack failed when it ran into alert German units near Fort Capuzzo. The 4th RTR lost a number of tanks and was forced to withdraw but that evening taught them another new lesson. Attempts by the regiment to recover some of its knocked-out tanks were frustrated by the Germans; the British managed to destroy some by setting them alight but that was the best for which they could hope. However, late that night sentries reported noises from the battlefield and in the morning it became clear that the Germans had recovered most of the least damaged British tanks. Many reports pay tribute to the efficiency of German recovery techniques throughout the desert war.

In the following month, with a fresh supply of tanks from Britain which were rushed at some risk through the Mediterranean, Operation Battleaxe was launched. For this 6th RTR was equipped with the first batch of newly arrived Crusader tanks; they were no better armed than earlier British cruisers but a good deal faster. Rommel, meanwhile, had received reinforcements in the form of 15th Panzer Division but he was still outnumbered by British tanks. He managed to redress this by using anti-tank guns and, in particular, a few 88-mm anti-aircraft guns which were devastating against British tanks.

C Squadron of 4th RTR lost all but one of its Matildas when attacking the head of Halfaya Pass without artillery support. Well-sited 88-mm guns and other German artillery brought the attack to a halt with heavy casualties. Battleaxe was an action of mixed fortunes, fought like a giant melée over the desert west of Sollum. The main thrust, by 7th Armoured Division, came unstuck for a variety of reasons which included inexperience, faulty intelligence and the mirage, but a shortage of radios did not help. In retrospect it has been claimed that in highly mobile tank fighting the British had the edge, pressing home the attack and firing on the move where German and Italian tanks preferred to stand off and shoot at the halt. When it was over, however, Rommel held the field. Indeed he practised an important tactical move which he continued to use in future battles. This involved going deep into the desert in order to sweep around the exposed British flank and it worked nearly every time.

The impact of Rommel's success may be gauged by the massive reinforcements despatched to North Africa from Britain. Three more infantry divisions and ten armoured regiments arrived in Egypt. Most were equipped with Crusaders but there was one with Valentine infantry tanks, while three of the existing regiments received American-built M3 light tanks, known as Honeys or General Stuarts by the British – the first Lend-Lease tanks to see service with the Royal Armoured Corps. Rommel, by contrast, was provided with a modest number of new tanks and told that his 5th Light Division should now restyle itself 21st Panzer Division. His most useful acquisition was an increased number of the excellent 5-cm anti-tank gun, the PAK 38.

In Cairo Wavell was now replaced by General Claude Auchinleck. Both sides needed time to prepare for further action and Rommel had a scheme for a major assault on Tobruk at the end of November. Auchinleck beat him by six days with a new offensive, known as Crusader, which was aimed at relieving Tobruk but with the prime intention of destroying as much German armour as possible. Although British intelligence would admit to a superiority in numbers over the combined Italian and German forces it still seriously overestimated the enemy's strength. In addition the mystique that surrounded Rommel credited him with such powers that his threat was perceived everywhere,

with the result that British units were continually calling for tank support and drawing them away from their main objectives.

With the Indian and New Zealand Divisions masking Axis garrisons in Sollum and Bardia, 7th Armoured Division executed a wide sweep west and north which brought the German armour to action around the airfield of Sidi Rezegh, south of Tobruk. Thus began an epic tank battle that raged for six days. Tank casualties on both sides were massive but the German anti-tank guns reduced the British advantage to the point where Rommel believed that British 30 Corps, at Sidi Rezegh, was now destroyed. He therefore decided to set off on a long-distance raid behind the British lines which he hoped would result in a general retreat. In fact he was wrong: 30 Corps was still a force to be reckoned with and his gallant drive achieved little. He missed two huge British Field Maintenance Areas, stocked with supplies, and came close to being caught himself during the second night.

Meanwhile the garrison from Tobruk had broken out and the siege was raised, but fighting began again at Sidi Rezegh and went on for three more days. It resulted in a serious reverse for the New Zealand Division and for a while Tobruk was cut off again, but the Axis forces were now so depleted that Rommel could afford no more losses and decided to withdraw, leaving behind a garrison trapped in Bardia. His final riposte, against British 4th Armoured Brigade at Bir el Gubi, had to be called off for lack of support from the Italian Mobile Corps and by early December he was occupying a defensive line running south from the coastal settlement of Gazala. Outflanked in the now traditional method from the south, Rommel, having picked up some extra tanks newly delivered to Benghazi, pulled back again to Agedabia, the limit of the British advance in 1940. Here, at the end of December, he turned on his pursuers and inflicted severe punishment on 22nd Armoured Brigade at El Haselat in which the British lost sixty-five tanks. Everyone was back more or less where they had started.

Bardia fell to a night attack on 1 January 1942. There remained a number of enemy posts in an area now totally dominated by British forces. One was the vital position of Halfaya Pass. An attack scheduled for 18 January never took place because the enemy surrendered, having run out of supplies. However, if anyone believed that they were in for a period of rest they underestimated Rommel.

An A13 Cruiser in a domestic desert scene. During long periods of inactivity, on operations, crews soon learned how to make the best of things. In this case a tent has been erected alongside the tank with boxes for seats set out in front. On the other side a loaded washing line completes the picture. One is forced to ask where the crew might have found so much spare water in such a barren spot.

One of Rommel's dummy tanks, assembled on light car chassis at a German Army workshop just established about 3 miles south of Tripoli. Rommel himself claims that they were produced in large numbers and that they were 'deceptively like the original', which obviously depends upon how close one got. The Volkswagen was powered by a four-cylinder, horizontally opposed, air-cooled engine.

A crew from 6th RTR with its temporary mount, an Italian M13/40 Medium Tank, which appears to have been repainted in the British light stone colour. The M13/40 was powered by a 105 hp diesel engine but it was hardly any faster than a Matilda while the armour was thin and brittle; it was also bolted onto a frame, which made it liable to break off under the impact of a shell.

Soon after he arrived in Tripoli Rommel undertook a number of personal reconnaissance flights to familiarize himself with the area. These revealed quite a lot of British activity around El Agheila and Agedabia which, in Rommel's view, presaged a further advance on Tripoli. Here a couple of troops of British A13 Cruiser tanks fan out across the desert.

Rommel's reaction to these British moves was to have his own units appear as active as possible too. Third Reconnaissance Battalion, along with the 39th Anti-tank Battalion and the Italian Battalion Santa Maria were ordered to head for Nofilia and make contact with British forces. Here a column of the Volkswagen-based dummy tanks moves out, heading away from the camera into the desert.

A picture which suggests the destruction of a British supply dump. Infantry in greatcoats can be seen entrenched in the foreground with others dangerously close to the explosion. An A9 or A10 Cruiser tank is in the centre with a Light Mark VI to its right while the two lorries are typical Canadian-built models. Shortage of time, more than of transport, meant that vast quantities of valuable stores had to be destroyed if they were not to fall into enemy hands.

The same went for tanks. If they broke down, and could not be repaired in time, they had to be rendered inoperative. The easiest way to achieve that was by blowing off the turret. In this case the victim is an ex-Italian M13/40 Medium and it is interesting to note that its temporary owners had gone to all the trouble of painting it in the latest British camouflage scheme and embellishing it with the Knight's Helm badge of 2nd Armoured Division.

Although probably not of a Long Range Desert Group vehicle, since it appears to be a Ford and carries an Arm of Service sign at the front, this picture has been included since it typifies their style and is of considerable rarity value. The body is a crude wooden structure and there are no doors, but a Browning machine-gun has been fitted for emergency use.

An abandoned Panzer II with the turret hatch open and engine covers up. The digits on the turret indicate the 3rd tank of the 4th troop of the 3rd company in a Panzer regiment while the letter R specifies a regimental officer's tank, suggesting that this one was serving in a command role. The Panzer II was powered by a six-cylinder Maybach petrol engine and its main armament was a 20-mm cannon.

A Panzer II of being unloaded from a merchant ship in Tripoli harbour. It bears the markings of 3rd Panzer Division, elements of which ultimately became 21st Panzer Division. When it came to reinforcing their army in Africa the Germans had the advantage, in military terms, of internal lines of communication. Tanks could be loaded onto trains in Germany and taken off at the dockside in southern Italy without ever passing through disputed territory.

An A9, or Cruiser Tank Mark I, stands guard at the approaches to the Derna Pass, February 1941. It is fitted with a 3.7-in close-support howitzer in place of the normal 40-mm gun. Such tanks were issued to regimental headquarters and, although the gun was capable of firing a high-explosive round, it was mainly supplied with smoke rounds.

Tanks used in the defence of the Tobruk perimeter were either dug in or otherwise protected from air attack. In this case the nearest one is partly surrounded by a low stone breastwork. The object was to maintain them and their crews well forward so that they could respond quickly to sudden attacks. The tanks shown here are A9 and A10 Cruisers.

Two knocked-out Matildas of 4th RTR with the grave of a crew member in the foreground. Although virtually invulnerable to most enemy anti-tank guns they could be disabled if their tracks were broken, as is the case here. Whether this was achieved by mines or gunfire is not clear but one imagines the crewman was killed after abandoning his tank.

A newly arrived Crusader is winched onto the back of a Scammell tank transporter. This rear view shows a number of interesting features: the rack across the back for spare fuel and water cans, the exposed engine air filters at the rear of each track guard and the so-called 'sunshine roof' turret hatch which had a nasty habit of sliding forward when least expected and injuring the commander.

A German 88-mm anti-aircraft gun in the travelling position behind its towing vehicle. If each of the rings on the barrel represents a kill this one has been very busy indeed. Rommel had employed these devastating weapons against tanks in France but in the desert they became the mainstay of his anti-tank armoury.

Two of 4th RTR's Matildas knocked out at Halfaya Pass. The tank at the bottom of the slope is still intact but the other has been entirely destroyed. The turret lies upside-down in the foreground; the other components are the left-side frame, suspension and some of the track. Even if all the ammunition went off at once it could hardly cause such destruction as this. It suggests a deliberate demolition job.

Crew members leap aboard their Valentine. Designed by Vickers-Armstrong as an infantry tank, the Valentine was slow but extremely reliable, which is more than can be said for most of its British contemporaries. It was armed with the standard British 2-pdr (40-mm) gun which, unfortunately, was incapable of firing a high-explosive round. Such a round would have proved very useful in the desert.

A desert meeting between a Morris Light Armoured Car, probably of the King's Dragoon Guards, fraternizing with an RTR Stuart. The Morris must be one of the last survivors by this time and it was probably being used as a headquarters vehicle. The Stuart, by comparison, is a new arrival. It was classed as a light tank but in most respects conformed to the specifications of a British cruiser.

A distant view of the battlefield at Sidi Rezegh, viewed over the turret of a 5th RTR Stuart. Tanks can be seen in the distance, with the occasional shell exploding beyond. Rare pictures such as this, while devoid of detail, do give a stark impression of what desert warfare was like. Distant tanks might belong to either side and even at this range, where the land is as flat as a billiard table stray shots could still pose a threat.

A remarkable snapshot taken through a turret periscope of a Crusader. Notice how a vertical strip on the vision block lines up with a vane, and that again matches the centre line of the gun barrel. This is how the tank's commander drew an initial bead on a target. Through the periscope one can see another Crusader and beyond that a line of tents and transport. The regiment is 3rd County of London Yeomanry of 22nd Armoured Brigade.

A poor picture but a striking illustration of the confusion at Sidi Rezegh. Manoeuvring in the dark a Crusader of 5th RTR has run full tilt into the side of an A10 Cruiser, disabling both tanks for the duration. Accidents like this probably happened quite frequently in an armoured melée. The driver's view is restricted anyway and in the heat of battle ordinary traffic rules do not apply. In the morning light tow ropes have been attached to the Crusader so that it could be towed clear.

Crusader tanks of A Squadron, 3rd County of London Yeomanry at rest. Each crew has rigged a large tent against the side of its tank. The raised wireless aerials, each displaying a pennant, suggest that this is a midday rest with the tanks keeping wireless watch. The regiment's first action, at Bir El Gubi on 18 November, resulted in severe casualties following an ill-advised attack.

A photograph taken near Derna on 22 December 1941 in the wake of Rommel's retreat to Benghazi. This Stuart, bearing the markings of 7th Armoured Division, has been hit, setting off an internal explosion that has lifted off the turret and turned it over. Few crew members would be expected to survive an inferno like this and the soldier in the foreground appears to be tending a grave.

Men of the Long Range Desert Group, their vehicles parked on the right, inspect an Italian M13/40 tank abandoned in Benghazi on 29 December 1941. The tank appears to have lost a suspension unit from the right side. Rommel had not only managed to withdraw all his troops to Agedabia by Christmas Day, he had also successfully removed all his supplies from Benghazi at the same time, leaving the British little more than the odd damaged tank.

A Matilda tank, buried up to turret-ring level, which formed part of the German defences at Capuzzo, on the Libyan border. This photograph was actually taken in 1942 but it seems very likely that this was one of the 4th RTR tanks knocked out at Halfaya Pass. Although it would appear to be a denial of the mobility of a tank this was one way in which older or disabled tanks could still find a useful role. The turrets of smaller tanks from this period were easy enough to operate manually and, dug in, they presented a tiny target.

CHAPTER 3
THE GAZALA LINE

The habit of underestimating Rommel seems to have been bequeathed by Wavell to his successor, General Auchinleck. The Auk had every intention of following up his present advantage by pushing on to Tripoli but first he had to build up his resources – and so, he believed, did Rommel. In the meantime the newly arrived 1st Armoured Division was moved out to cover the Agedabia–El Haselat area with its three tank regiments comprising 2nd Armoured Brigade. Rommel himself had been reinforced to the tune of about fifty tanks, but very few officers, even on his own side, believed that he was in a fit state to renew the offensive.

But he did. On 21 January 1942, after air reconnaissance had revealed the weakness of British positions, he broke through the immediate opposition and two days later encountered the British armour with which he dealt harshly. From there, as now was becoming traditional, he was faced with the choice of routes eastwards: around the coast or direct via Msus and Mechili. Appearing to choose the latter he went halfway to Msus and then swung back to take Benghazi, which was held by 4th Indian Division. Rommel met tough opposition in places but it was as nothing compared to what his own side was trying to do. The German High Command was nervous and his Italian allies effectively refused to join in, thereby placing his entire plan in jeopardy. Not that he had any long-term plans. Rommel invariably sought to take advantage of a situation for as long as it seemed profitable; he pushed hard but remained flexible and seems to have had an instinct for his enemy's reactions.

On the British side there was no one individual with this kind of intuition. General Ritchie, Auchinleck's commander on the spot, persisted in believing that Rommel would not be able to sustain his advance and, on his own initiative, almost condemned the Indian Division to investment, if not capture, in Benghazi. Rommel's subsequent moves continued to sow confusion among the British commanders and a series of proposed defence lines had to be abandoned until the Allies were back on the Gazala Line, which Rommel had attempted to defend the year before. However, Ritchie and Auchinleck were ambivalent about a defence line. In the first place they were not intending to remain on the defensive so the positions were planned more as a jumping-off point for future attacks. Secondly, the fortified positions, or 'Boxes', which comprised the Gazala Line were well spaced out, especially at the southern end, too well spaced out for mutual support although, unlike the Italian positions in Egypt in 1940, the gaps between them were covered with minefields. Again, because it was regarded as a position from which a counter-attack might be mounted, the Gazala Line did not have its defences in depth. There were just two significant rearward positions: Acroma in the north and Knightsbridge a short distance to the south, which covered vital junctions on supply routes from the east.

Ritchie had the best part of four months to prepare and improve his position at Gazala since Rommel had already achieved more than he had the resources to exploit and was obliged to hold fast. Auchinleck made no attempt to seize the initiative, despite tremendous pressure from London. To Churchill and the War Cabinet it was beyond understanding. Men and equipment had been poured into the desert and they expected results. Russia was being hammered while her Allies appeared to be doing nothing and Malta was exposed to continual enemy bombing which could have been eased if the Desert Air Force could only get back to the airfields it had used in northern Cyrenaica,

which the Luftwaffe was now using. Auchinleck understood the situation but he was determined not to move until he was ready. In the end he was given a direct order but, before he could act upon it, Rommel struck.

On 27 May five Italian divisions posed a threat along the entire length of the Gazala Line. While all Allied eyes gazed west a huge motorized force comprising three armoured divisions, two German and one Italian, with thousands of supply and troop-carrying vehicles, swung round the southern end of the line and headed north. Rommel directed most of his armour to Acroma but out on the flank his 90th Light Division made towards Tobruk, using lorries equipped with aircraft engines to kick up the dust and give an impression of even more armour in the offing.

Sweeping British units aside, the massive German column rolled on until it fell upon 4th Armoured Brigade early the next morning. The three regiments of this brigade had recently been re-equipped with the new American M3 Grant tanks, each regiment having sufficient Grants for two squadrons. The Grant was not ideal, with its main armament located in the hull, but it was reliable compared with most British tanks and much harder hitting. As the Germans soon discovered to their dismay, the Grant's 75-mm gun could damage their tanks before they could get within range to hit back, but that was not the only surprise. As already mentioned the Germans always operated tanks in close cooperation with anti-tank guns. It was a practice the British came to envy since such joint action was not common in their divisions. However, the Germans in North Africa had now developed this a stage further to the extent that, during an attack, tanks and anti-tank guns leapfrogged one another as they advanced. This not only ensured mutual support, it also subjected the enemy to more constant fire and added to their difficulties. Against an enemy tank the normal practice was to fire armour-piercing ammunition, which in those days was generally solid shot, but this was not a lot of use against anti-tank guns. The 5-cm PAK 38, for example, was a minuscule target compared with a tank and the chances of hitting it were slim. Far better to drop a high-explosive round close to it in the hope that if one did not incapacitate the crew, at least they would be distracted. The problem was that until the arrival of the Grant no British tank had the capability to fire high-explosive and armour-piercing rounds from the same gun.

There is no doubt that the presence of these new American tanks, known originally as *Pilots* by the Germans who misunderstood a photo caption, upset Rommel's plans, but he managed to shoulder the three regiments aside and continue his advance. It is more unfortunate for the British that they had failed to bring more of their armour together before Rommel struck because he then caused similar damage to 22nd Armoured Brigade and that night he was close to Acroma. By the next morning more British armour was moving towards the action and Rommel had cause for concern. His 15th Panzer Division was running out of ammunition and 90th Light Division, recalled from its eastern adventure, was suffering from ground and air attacks. Once he got his forces together Rommel formed a defensive position for the night.

The British did not press home their advantage at once, and worse still they failed to prevent Rommel himself from venturing out to locate his supply column and guide it to the tanks. Thus the next morning the Germans were ready to renew the fight. In fact they got two days of relative peace which enabled Rommel to move his armour to a more defensible site although he now had a British Box and minefields between him and the west. The respite was caused in part by a succession of sandstorms but mainly by indecision among British commanders as to the best course to adopt next. Rommel had no such problem. When no British assault came in he attacked west, destroyed the adjacent 150 Brigade Box at Sidi Muftah and cleared a route to the west. Next he turned his troops on the southernmost Box at Bir Hacheim, occupied by the Free French, which proved such a tough nut that it took nine days to crack; however, in the meantime the Panzers were back in action.

The area from which Rommel operated had become known as the 'Cauldron' and it was here, on 5 June, that Ritchie elected to destroy the German armour. The area saw some of the most intense tank fighting so far. Unfortunately the British threw in their ingredients one after another, only to have them destroyed or repulsed piecemeal, and within twenty-four hours the Allies had sacrificed their advantage. For the next few days action was spasmodic but when the Free French were driven out of Bir Hachiem on 10 June Rommel felt free to resume his advance. Considering the risks he had run and the hammering he had taken this was all but incredible. He had lost tanks that he could not replace and although the British had lost many more they had reinforcements on the way. Yet by 12 June Rommel had managed to trap and seriously damage two British armoured brigades before turning his attention to the Knightsbridge position on 13 June. That he did not find this easy was attributable in no small part to the efforts of the 7th/42nd RTRs (a number of temporary amalgamations had taken place as a result of losses among tanks and crews) commanded by Lieutenant-Colonel H.R.B. Foote who was awarded the Victoria Cross for this and other brilliant efforts.

On 14 June Ritchie gave the order to abandon the Gazala Line. Many units and even divisions had hair-raising escapes since a considerable part of Rommel's army was already between them and their intended destination, but like the surviving British tank crews their German counterparts were simply too exhausted to engage in a vigorous pursuit. Auchinleck had instructed Ritchie to fall back in line with El Adem and Tobruk, but the latter ordered his troops back to the frontier and in doing so created another problem. In plans made earlier, before Rommel's attack, it had been agreed that in the event of retreat Tobruk would not be held through another siege since it was not considered practical. As it was, in the scramble to escape after Gazala some of the British armour had withdrawn into the Tobruk perimeter and once again the decision was taken to remain there.

Since most histories of the desert war concentrate on the main armoured battles it might not be out of place here to make some mention of the armoured cars and their invaluable work. As we have already seen, the 11th Hussars made some significant contributions to the early success as they continued to do throughout the campaign. They were soon joined by the King's Dragoon Guards and other British regiments and the South Africans. The South African Tank Corps was formed in 1940 and gained early combat experience in Abyssinia and East Africa, almost entirely in armoured cars, many of which were little better than home made. The Union Defence Force was founded with the intention of protecting the homeland and there was some doubt concerning its authority to operate further afield. Inevitably, however, this valuable force became a fully committed element in the Allied armies and in the summer of 1941 was preparing for service in the Middle East. This grew to the point where the South African Army had two armoured reconnaissance battalions and three armoured car regiments in the desert, mainly equipped with Marmon-Herrington armoured cars built in South Africa on imported American chassis.

By the time the South Africans were operational with Eighth Army the role of armoured car regiments had become established. Patrols might be sent out to cover a front of 40 miles or more, setting up observation points which reported back on whatever they were able to see through the shimmering heat haze and mirage. Reports were channelled through squadron headquarters to rear link signal vehicles which relayed them to higher command. With all sets tuned to a common net it was possible for all units to remain aware of the wider situation and thus build up a complete picture. However, in the heat of battle the armoured cars were in constant demand. They would be required to dash all over the field in search of information which was often gathered at considerable risk, and it is an unfortunate consequence of the unsettled nature of such battles that their reports were not always believed. Finally, when a battle ended as Gazala did, the armoured cars formed a rearguard, rounding up stragglers and hitting back at the enemy whenever they got the chance.

The driver of an A10 (Cruiser Mark II) of 1st Armoured Division, resplendent in his new pith helmet, chats to local troops on arrival in Egypt. The division had taken quite a battering in France and abandoned all its tanks there. In Britain it was provided with replacements, but stocks were low and many of the tanks now arriving in Egypt were not just past their prime, they were rapidly being outclassed by new German types.

Crowds gather at the docks in Tripoli to watch German tanks moving out into the desert. The officer in the foreground turns to watch a Panzer II which is following a Panzer III along the quay. Both tanks appear to be finished in the European dark grey, indicating that they have only recently arrived in North Africa. Towering over the whole scene is one of those ostentatious monuments that Mussolini was so fond of erecting all over Libya.

Acclimatizing to desert conditions was not just a matter of learning to soak up the sunshine. Huge sandstorms could sweep across the country, inflicting misery on everyone. Here, during the German advance, tents bulge in the wind while blown sand reduces visibility to a few yards. The Panzer II in the foreground is undoubtedly closed down, but the sand will get in anyway.

Although the Indians did not have an armoured division in the desert, they did operate armoured, wheeled carriers, designed in India and mounted on Canadian Ford four-wheel drive chassis. They were armed only with light machine-guns and anti-tank rifles and were used for reconnaissance, liaison and general security duties in the infantry division.

During a hasty retreat a breakdown can spell disaster. There is rarely time to organize repairs and everyone else is in a great hurry to get away. This British Stuart appears to be receiving help from a Scammell recovery vehicle although the crew does not seem to be imbued with that sense of urgency which one might expect if the Germans were in hot pursuit.

German and Italian soldiers guard a disconsolate group of British prisoners. In desert conditions, where the first priority for everyone was survival, an escape attempt was not to be undertaken lightly, but there were those who were prepared to chance it. Rommel himself recounts the tale of one troublesome British prisoner, while the history of the Indian divisions in Libya contains some amazing accounts.

A British 2-pdr anti-tank gun which has taken at least one small-calibre hit on its shield. The token breastwork of stones would appear to be worse than useless for anything more than decoration and it is interesting to compare it with German practice. A Panzer IV can be seen in the middle distance.

A Crusader is hurried forward on an American-built White tank transporter. Notice that the crew travel with their tank. These six-wheeled transporters were not popular with tank crews who felt that they were unstable. The narrow loading ramps, seen stowed beneath the tank, were steep and difficult to climb and it was even worse trying to get off.

A copy of a German snapshot, picked up by a British soldier in the desert. It shows a group of men, probably from a reconnaissance unit, posing alongside a Horch heavy field car. The ever ready MG 34 machine-gun, on its anti-aircraft mounting, illustrates the constant threat of air attack to which everyone was exposed. Notice, in the background, how other vehicles are widely spaced out to prevent an air strike from claiming too many victims at once.

An Italian reconnaissance patrol moving out into the desert. These armoured cars, or *Autoblindata*, were among the best Italian armoured vehicles of the war. Equipped with four-wheel drive and powered by a 100 bhp petrol engine they featured a six-speed gearbox which functioned in either direction, enabling them to get out of a difficult situation in a hurry without turning round.

The hazards of reconnaissance. The crew of a German Sd Kfz 222 armoured car are laid to rest beneath improvised crosses alongside their damaged vehicle. These scout cars, which carried a 20-mm gun, were large by British standards and should probably be compared more accurately with a British armoured car.

M3 Grant tanks, all on transporters, in the desert. American instructors are going through the technical details with the new British crews before handing them over. There were problems with the American tanks, notably vapour lock in the engines and rubber peeling off the road wheels in the heat, but in general British crews found them vastly more reliable than British types and there is no doubt that they appreciated the 75-mm gun.

A British soldier gazes rather vacantly at a captured German 5-cm anti-tank gun. At 1,000 yd it could penetrate 50 mm of armour and it was extremely accurate, but its greatest advantage was the remarkably low silhouette. This made it a very difficult target to spot in the turmoil of battle and even harder to hit, especially for a British tank which was unable to fire high-explosive rounds.

Crusaders forming up for an attack. Action is not imminent, for the commanders are sitting well out of their turrets, but even when the shot did start flying around most British tank commanders preferred to keep the hatches open and their heads out. This was not just bravado; it made observation easier and provided an instant means of escape if the tank was hit.

A knocked-out A13 Cruiser of 1st Armoured Division alongside a wrecked German Panzer I surrounded by all kinds of debris after an intense battle. This gives some idea of the nature of fighting within the Cauldron where close and sudden action was the rule. This was rather to the advantage of the British whose tank crews were trained to shoot accurately on the move.

British transport passing the still burning wreck of an Italian tank. Fire in a tank was dreaded by crews of all nationalities. It was more likely to start in the ammunition than the fuel and this meant that it began in the crew area. The chances of everyone getting out alive were slim and it was a disagreeable task for those who had to deal with the remains.

A Panzer IV burning near Tobruk. This is a fuel fire which may well have been started deliberately to disable it. The tank mounts a short 75-mm weapon, primarily intended for close support work but capable of firing anti-tank projectiles. The extra road wheels attached to hull and turret are carried primarily as replacements but the spare track is mainly used for additional protection.

Since the Germans were renowned for their ability to recover and repair damaged tanks the Royal Engineers did their best to wreck them thoroughly. In this case they might have overdone it. The entire superstructure and turret have been blown clear off this Panzer III. The crew of the British Universal Carrier have probably just stopped to have a look.

A Matilda on the edge of the battlefield. Moving in easy stages from one battle to another these ponderous infantry tanks found themselves operating hundreds of miles away from Egypt, with little prospect of returning if things went against them. A top speed of 15 mph, which could not be sustained for long, did not improve their chances of escape. Behind the Matilda is what appears to be a portee vehicle which would normally be carrying an anti-tank gun.

A scene which must have been repeated often during the British withdrawal. The driver of a Bedford 15-cwt platoon truck stops to photograph a group of abandoned and burning vehicles. The surrounding air is thick with dust, no doubt in this case thrown up by other retreating vehicles. In such conditions it is not surprising that both sides could miss one another by a few yards, or meet suddenly.

Once again vast stocks of stores had to be destroyed to prevent them from falling into enemy hands. As part of the plan to sustain an advance to Tripoli the British had created vast supply dumps, called Forward Maintenance Areas, which were constantly restocked by transport columns, at hidden locations in the desert. The fuel and food they contained, if not the ammunition, would be of immense value to the enemy.

Although taken before the war this picture illustrates one of the most vital items ever devised for desert navigation: the sun compass. Working roughly on the sun-dial principle it featured a series of interchangeable discs covering specific locations and time periods which the user fitted as required. Major Ralph Bagnold undertook much of the development work before the war.

Humber armoured cars of the 11th Hussars on patrol. They were four-wheel drive, rear-engined types armed with a pair of Besa machine-guns, one 7.62-mm and one 15-mm. Being a desert-wise regiment the Cherrypickers adorned their cars with pretty well everything the desert traveller might need for comfort and it was always said of the Eighth Army that its vehicles looked more like tinkers' carts than combat machines.

An aerial view of a Marmon-Herrington Mark II armoured car, taken for recognition purposes. This one sports the geometric, three-colour, disruptive camouflage pattern known as the Caunter Scheme. It mounts a Boys rifle and Bren gun in the turret with a mounting for a Vickers on the back. The chevrons on the bonnet are designed to deflect shot away from the driver's visor and there are sand channels stowed across the rear wheels.

Heavily camouflaged against observation from the air a Marmon-Herrington sits out in the desert on picket duty. Very little of the vehicle can be seen and the wireless aerial has been folded down to reduce visibility. Even so all the weapons, including the water-cooled Vickers machine-gun on the back of the turret, are clear of obstruction and ready in the event of an air attack.

CHAPTER 4
THE DEFENCE OF EGYPT

With General Ritchie anxious to get his forces back across the Egyptian frontier, and Rommel hard on his heels, it was obvious that Tobruk was in for another spell of investment. Following a rapid exchange of tanks 4th and 7th RTR found themselves inside the garrison with most of the surviving Matildas, some of which were provided with dugouts in which to hide or from which to fight. Auchinleck's desire to avoid a second siege was matched by Rommel who now threw as much weight as he could spare against the town and soon captured it.

Meanwhile Ritchie, believing the frontier to be indefensible because of its vulnerability to an outflanking attack from the south, now pulled back to a line running south from Mersah Matruh on which he expected to be left in peace to recruit his strength. The fact that it was just as vulnerable to one of Rommel's patent attacks seems to have been discounted on the grounds that the enemy must be too exhausted to follow through. Rommel, however, was on a roll and while the situation remained fluid he had every

expectation of pursuing the disorganized Allies all the way to Alexandria. Thus, by the end of June 1942 the situation was almost farcical.

The German 90th Light Division was already well beyond Mersa Matruh, aiming to cut the coast road 30 miles to the east. On their right 21st Panzer Division was poised to sweep around behind 2nd New Zealand Division from the north while 15th Panzer Division attacked from the west. South of them again the Italian Ariete and Trieste divisions were also moving east. Rommel's intention was to clear up the southernmost British positions to give himself a clear run to the Delta but he was moving into an area occupied by most of the surviving British armour which was still endeavouring to counter-attack westwards. The result was a series of running fights in which the Germans maintained the advantage and created havoc. Rather than assist the New Zealanders the British armour was ordered to withdraw and the Kiwis had to fight their own way out, as did the garrison at Mersah Matruh, so one had the ridiculous situation of British troops and their Allies retreating east in company with German columns bent on capturing Egypt. The difference was that the German and Italian forces had this objective and destination in mind while the Allies had no idea where they were supposed to be going.

In fact the British intention was to establish another line, running south from the railway halt of El Alamein, where the gap between the Qattara Depression and the sea was at its narrowest and where a succession of ridges, running east–west, would tend to channel Rommel's attacks. Not that much was expected. The Afrika Korps was, for a while, down to fewer than thirty operational tanks, its supply lines were stretched to the limit and the RAF, operating from close to home, was posing a serious threat. Typically the Alamein line was not continuous. It comprised four Boxes, two occupied by Indian brigades and one each by South African and New Zealand forces. The gaps between them were theoretically covered by mobile support columns which, on 1 July when Rommel attacked, were not yet fully organized. Thus when one of the Indian Boxes was attacked the British armour took much too long to react and the position had been overwhelmed before the tanks arrived.

The next day Rommel planned to renew his attack while Auchinleck had his own scheme ready. Neither succeeded and, bearing in mind that everyone was exhausted, it might not be too unfair to say that soldiers on both sides were becoming somewhat hesitant in the attack.

Certainly on the British side the reputation of the armour was at its lowest. The infantry, and in particular the Commonwealth troops, now openly expressed their lack of confidence in the ability of the tanks to help them. It was noticeable that, after three days of fighting on the El Alamein line, German and Italian troops became jumpy when attacked, while on the British side orders issued with considerable vigour by the Commander-in-Chief were so watered down by the time they reached the front line troops that they were not acted upon with sufficient enthusiasm and many opportunities were lost.

Although Auchinleck managed to sustain attacks sufficient to hold Rommel in check he was faced with the problem that the northernmost of the east–west ridges, known as Ruweisat Ridge, was in enemy hands. This feature became the focal point of a succession of attacks and counter-attacks right up to the end of the month, culminating in an action which, for sheer desperation, seems to epitomize the Allied situation. Newly arrived in Egypt, the 23rd Armoured Brigade, comprising the 40th, 46th and 50th RTRs, was a territorial brigade equipped primarily with Valentines. The situation being serious the brigade did not have the normal opportunities to acclimatize. It arrived in Egypt on 6 July and was drawn up to drive the Germans off Ruweisat Ridge on 22 July. Lack of experience was more than balanced by enthusiasm, and there are those who suggest that it was a cynical move on the part of the British High Command, designed to counteract the jaded attitude of the desert veterans.

The battle began with a reverse for the Allied infantry, which meant that the tanks went in alone and the support they were expecting from 22nd Armoured Brigade was not forthcoming. They ran smack into a well-prepared defence, the inevitable mixture of tanks and anti-tank guns. Both 40th and 46th RTR were nearly wiped out. The 50th, operating on the flank, had an equally hard time. In all the brigade lost 118 tanks while the Germans lost just 3.

Things had reached such a pass by the end of July that the Prime Minister flew out to Egypt with the intention of making a clean sweep of the British command. Sir Harold Alexander was to replace Auchinleck and General 'Strafer' Gott was appointed to command the Eighth Army. There were changes at Corps level too. Unfortunately Gott died in an air crash the day after his appointment and at very short notice the position was given to General Montgomery who, up to that time, was expecting a command in Tunisia. One reason why Churchill got rid of Auchinleck was the latter's refusal to contemplate a new offensive before September. Yet the new team of Alexander and Montgomery could hardly expect to move much faster, especially with another German offensive pending.

It opened on 30 August with the usual Rommel tactic of a swing around the southern end of the Allied line. On this occasion the 90th Light Division, along with the Italian XXth Corps, made a bee-line once again for the long-suffering 2nd New Zealand Division while the Afrika Korps swung wide and headed north for the coast road. There, however, the similarity ended. British armoured regiments were now equipped with a healthy number of Grant tanks but they refused to be drawn out into the open. Launched at night, Rommel's attack was first slowed and then diverted when the British minefields turned out to be deeper than expected. Lurking behind the mines British tanks continued to harry the advancing Germans who were unable to get at them.

Moving north in daylight the German plan was now to take the Alam Halfa Ridge, the eminence south of Ruweisat Ridge, but here they ran into Grant tanks well established in good defensive positions and were brought to a halt. For two days Rommel continued the attack but every attempt to outflank was countered and he was under constant bombardment from artillery and the RAF. Finally, with just twenty-four hours reserve of fuel remaining, he ordered a slow retreat. An attempt to cut him off failed and Montgomery was reluctant to commit his tanks to a pursuit lest Rommel should catch them in the open and turn the tables. It was already clear that the Germans had a new weapon, in the shape of a Panzer IV tank with a long and devastating 75-mm gun. These Panzer IV Specials, as the British called them, were quite capable of dealing with the Grant and it was a mercy that for this battle Rommel could only muster twenty-seven of them.

The ground below the Alam Halfa Ridge marks the high point of the Afrika Korps' ambition to capture Egypt and the Suez Canal. Rommel was just 60 miles from Cairo but it was 60 miles he would never travel. Writing later Rommel admits that this defeat effectively cost him the chance of total success. His supply route across the Mediterranean was now more uncertain than ever while British resources were expanding at an alarming rate and there is no doubt at all that the heavy bombing raids, which continued day and night, were unwelcome. Added to which he was now dealing with a British commander who would not easily be lured into some rash action and then destroyed. Montgomery was far too cautious to provide Rommel with the opportunities he used to enjoy. All he could do now was to settle into the positions he had captured, strengthen them as far as possible and then await Montgomery's pleasure.

Despite the inevitable urging from London, Alexander and Montgomery agreed that they should postpone the offensive until they had overwhelming strength and newly arrived troops were properly acclimatized and trained. It would be a massive force that Rommel would have to face when the time came – sufficient artillery to produce an opening barrage of First World War proportions and an excellent new tank, in the shape of the Sherman. This American machine, based on the running gear of the M3

Grant, now mounted its 75-mm gun in a proper rotating turret. In addition to its firepower it was better protected than the earlier model and, like other American tanks, was far more reliable than any British type except, perhaps, the Valentine. A handful of the new Churchill infantry tanks would make their desert debut in Monty's battle and he had also increased numbers of a new model Crusader which had first appeared that summer. This type, the Crusader III, had the new 57-mm (6-pdr) gun in its turret which was a vast improvement on the 2-pdr but still incapable of firing a high-explosive round to any effect. Unfortunately the new model had a reduced crew, to accommodate the new gun and ammunition, which made it more tiring than ever to operate and, being a Crusader, it still suffered from the chronic unreliability which bedevilled the type.

The increasing use of minefields to deny ground and channel the route of an attack was probably the only way to create a tactical situation in an otherwise barren landscape. It was, however, a double-edged weapon. As the extent of the minefields expanded those that had provided protection from attack now became a hindrance to the advance and vice versa. The traditional method of clearing them, with teams working on foot to detect and lift each mine, was time-consuming, as Rommel had found during his attack on Alam Halfa, and dangerous, particularly when carried out under fire.

Tanks carrying mine-detonating rollers had already been developed but their effect was limited because a roller was destroyed with each mine, and after three, at most, the tank had to withdraw. Thus they were adequate for detecting the presence of a minefield but they were not able to clear it. Following suggestions from a South African officer a rotating flail attachment was devised which, barring bad luck, could clear a lane right through a minefield. Fitted to redundant Matilda tanks this equipment, christened Scorpion, was ready for service in time to take part in Montgomery's great offensive, scheduled to begin before dawn on 23 October 1942.

A Matilda dug in at Tobruk. Creating such a pit was hard work but worth it since, apart from its turret, the tank was well protected. It was still capable of fighting from this hull-down position but the tank can exit rapidly up the ramp at the back if it is required to counter-attack. The cover at the back suggests that the crew were living with their tank, ready for instant action.

The commander of a Panzer IV uses a set of periscope binoculars to calculate the range for his 75-mm gun. It was generally agreed that when it came to producing optical equipment the Germans were superior to all others and had a greater variety available. A set of liberated German binoculars was every soldier's ambition. Notice the memorial to a former crew member, killed in action, that has been painted on the hull gunner's side visor cover.

Two Humber armoured cars at a gap in the wire on the Libyan frontier. It would appear to be early morning. The crew are rolling up their bed rolls and preparing to stow them on the cars. The tracks leading away from the cars appear to have been neatly lined with stones, as is the little memorial column which looks as if it might be the centre of a small war grave plot.

Valentine tanks of 8th RTR near Bardia. They are finished in a two-tone camouflage scheme, probably a dark brick-red over sand. The stripes on the turret and sand skirts are the white/red/white markings which became a standard identification feature for British tanks in the desert.

A German SdKfz 251 armoured command vehicle and attendant despatch rider in the desert. The 251 was a half-track, designed originally as a troop carrier but adapted to a variety of roles. This version, SdKfz 251/3, came equipped with a range of radio sets and an Enigma decoding machine and they were easily recognizable by the large bedstead frame aerial and other antenna.

An RTR officer and his driver with their Daimler Dingo scout car. Although British tanks enjoyed a poor reputation at this time the humble Dingo was one of the best vehicles in its class, worldwide. It had a rear-mounted Daimler six-cylinder engine which drove all four wheels through a five-speed each-way gearbox and fluid flywheel. Being compact, fast and highly manoeuvrable it was the ideal reconnaissance vehicle.

Stuart and Grant tanks observing movement on the horizon. Although Rommel repeatedly employed outflanking tactics he could not disguise them for long. In conditions such as this, on ground as flat as a bowling green, all such moves are easily spotted by the dust they throw up, giving the defenders time to prepare. Rather than attempt to disguise this Rommel often did his best to make his force look more daunting than it was.

A knocked-out Panzer IV with a British Humber armoured car beyond. The device on top of the exhaust pipe on the German tank is designed to produce a smoke screen. Although it depended on weather conditions, smoke was a valuable asset on the battlefield. Allied tanks were provided with forward firing smoke dischargers and most tanks carried smoke shells as part of their ammunition complement.

A Crusader on outpost duty. Despite its unreliability the tank was popular for its high speed of nearly 30 mph. However, fitting the air cleaners outside the hull – one can be seen on the nearside rear track guard – did not help since they were easily damaged and became clogged with sand. The drum at the back was supposed to contain extra petrol but many crews preferred to fill it with water which they considered far more important and much less vulnerable.

Stuart tanks keep a watching brief in the evening. It is all too easy to overlook the fact that, even out of action, there was a great deal for tank crews to do. The tank itself had to be serviced and restocked with fuel and ammunition. The commander might have to attend a briefing and men would be needed for sentry duty at night or to keep radio watch. Any spare time was simply used to eat and sleep.

Although rarely photographed in the desert east of Tripoli, three of these Panzer III-based Sturmgeschutz Ausf. D self-propelled assault guns were employed at Gazala and Tobruk. A British regimental history records the capture of one which was chased by a Universal Carrier. This one is shown after capture at a British base in Egypt. It mounts a short 75-mm gun.

Photographed after capture this dug-in 88-mm gun is typical of those that defended the German positions on Ruweisat Ridge. Someone has placed a round on the edge of the pit. Seen like this it is easy to understand why British tank crews found the 'eighty-eights' so difficult to spot. One of these weapons, manned by Gunner Gunther Halm, accounted for nine Valentines during the Ruweisat action.

Valentines belonging to C Squadron, 46th RTR, knocked out in the Ruweisat Ridge battle of 22 July 1942. C Squadron fought on the left flank, attacking a point known as El Mireir where the German anti-tank screen was backed up by 15th Panzer Division. When the battle was over the whole area was littered with wrecked and smouldering tanks.

Prime Minister Churchill's visit to Eighth Army was a great success from the soldiers' point of view but bad news for Auchinleck. Here the Prime Minister is seen perched in a Morris-Commercial 8-cwt pick-up truck. Colonel E.I.C. Jacob records hearing Churchill say, 'Rommel, Rommel, Rommel, Rommel. What else matters but beating him?'

The new commander, General Montgomery, wearing a smart bush hat, inspects the ammunition on a South African armoured car. This Marmon-Herrington has been modified by removing the turret and mounting a 25-mm Hotchkiss anti-tank gun. Such modifications were extremely popular among Marmon-Herrington crews who, like most soldiers, believed their vehicle, as designed, was under-gunned.

A pair of Grants which, from their general state, appear to have been knocked out. Much as its reliability and good gun were appreciated the tank was so tall that many crews felt very exposed out on the desert. Another problem faced by the commander was handling the diverse armament. Being in the turret, with its 37-mm gun, he was liable to concentrate on its target rather than that of the hull-mounted 75-mm. A sensible commander relied on a good hull gunner, working in close harmony with the driver.

A Panzer IV Special, damaged and abandoned in the open desert. As an anti-tank gun the KwK 40, 75-mm, was second only in effect to the 88-mm. It was a measure of the good design of this tank that it was possible to up-gun the Panzer IV without spoiling its performance or reducing the crew. The side doors in the turret, a feature of Panzers III and IV, were a welcome source of ventilation in the desert but a weakness in the structural integrity of the turret shell.

Photographed in September 1942 this Panzer IV Special has been well and truly wrecked. An internal explosion has dislodged the superstructure and fire has destroyed the road wheel tyres. On the other side the track and some of the suspension appear to have gone along with the track guard. Rommel never had enough of these tanks to satisfy him and the Allies treated them with a great deal of respect.

A Scammell 30-ton tank transporter, with a Grant up, in the desert. The Scammell had a superb cross-country performance and the extended cab provided seating for the entire crew. However, the semi-trailer was not so popular. It was set at a steep angle and, particularly with a Grant on board, tended to become very top-heavy, especially when cornering on uneven ground. Designed originally for tank recovery these transporters were generally used for moving tank regiments in order to save wear on their tracks.

One of the very first Shermans to arrive at the main Eighth Army workshops in Egypt. It still has the shipping instructions painted on the hull. This is the type M4A1, with a cast hull, powered by a nine-cylinder, air-cooled radial engine which was known as the Sherman II in British service. Its 75-mm gun was no better than that of the Grant but it was mounted where it ought to be, in the turret. This tank is in the process of having sand shields fitted for desert service.

Strong man act. This White transporter has tipped up while unloading a Crusader, giving this joker his opportunity. The tank is the new Mark III Crusader, mounting the 57-mm, 6-pdr gun. It was a tight fit; the hull gunner was removed to make room for more ammunition and only two men could be accommodated in the turret, which made it much harder work for the remaining members of the crew.

Rearing up on its transporter, a Matilda tank fitted with anti-mine rollers prepares to be winched on board. In most cases, once a roller had detonated a mine it was also destroyed. Obviously once two rollers on one side had gone the tank could not proceed without risk so it would then jettison the frame and behave like an ordinary tank. Such machines were best employed in detecting minefields rather than in trying to clear them.

The best solution to mechanized mine clearing was the rotary flail, mounted on the front of a tank. This original model, fitted to the Matilda, was known as the Scorpion. It was powered by a separate engine, mounted in a box on the right side of the tank. This drove the rotating drum, causing the chain and wire flails to thrash the ground and explode any mines they hit.

CHAPTER 5
EL ALAMEIN

The battle known to history as El Alamein began on Friday 23 October 1942 and ran for nearly two weeks. Its significance is undeniable for although, as we have seen, Rommel had now consigned his plan to capture Egypt to the dustbin he had no intention of withdrawing tamely from the fray. That his ultimate fate was inevitable may be deduced from the statistics but results calculated from such figures are not always as clear cut as they should be. Comparing the figures for tanks, as published in the British *Official History* for instance, one finds the Allies credited with 1,029 fit for action and with their regiments on the eve of the battle, while the Germans and Italians between them had 547, plus another 20 under repair. Of these 51 were light tanks of little combat value and 7 were command tanks, while of the total Axis tank force 298 were Italian machines of an inferior type. The best tank on the battlefield at this time was undoubtedly the Panzer IV Special with its long 75-mm gun but Rommel only had 30 of them whereas its nearest Allied counterpart, the Sherman, was available in much larger numbers to Montgomery: the figure given is 252. In addition the British had some 300 armoured cars; the number available to the Germans is not known.

Juggle with these figures as one might it always spells a massive advantage to the British and their Allies, and this superiority can be extended to include infantry and artillery, the massive reserve of stores that Alexander and Montgomery had created behind the Allied lines and, of course, the Desert Air Force. Even so this preponderance of men and materials did not imply a walkover. A commander of Montgomery's deliberate style was not the kind to employ the daring flanking moves so beloved of Rommel and in any case the German commander had prepared against this by building his defensive line from the coast right to the edge of the Qattara Depression. Wherever he attacked Monty would have to hit the enemy head on, having first crossed some impressive minefields in the face of concentrated anti-tank fire. Addressing his commanders before the battle Montgomery made it clear that he anticipated a long, drawn-out fight.

Following a brief but well-prepared barrage of 1,000 guns the attack began at 10 p.m. under a full moon. Infantry, closely supported by Valentine tanks, began the task of clearing two corridors through the minefields to create routes for 1st and 10th Armoured Divisions. Rommel himself was in Europe for medical treatment but hastened back as soon as the news broke. Meanwhile his deputy, General Stumme, collapsed and died of a heart attack on the second day of the battle. For the British, progress through the minefields was slower than expected and it was 26 October before the two corridors were completed. A diversionary attack by 7th Armoured Division to the south failed but in the meantime the British armour had consolidated in the north and easily beat off enemy counter-attacks with tanks. At the same time Allied infantry cleared the gap between the two corridors and a brief rest period was called during which 7th Armoured Division replaced the 1st. However, it was now clear that with Rommel again in charge any attempt to continue along the present axis would be fiercely resisted.

Montgomery therefore altered his plans and struck north on 28 October with the intention of reaching the coast and splitting the enemy force. This was partly achieved by 1 November but Rommel countered the move and the Allied commanders switched their attack once again, along its original course. The Germans were now in a very difficult position. Ideally Rommel would have liked to have drawn back to a new position around Fuka but a lack of transport meant that he would be sacrificing too many of his troops if he did so. Even so his move north had not just thinned his original defensive line, but had also used up valuable reserves of fuel which were limited enough anyway. Despite this the Allies did not find their new attack an easy option. New minefields had appeared in front of them and the anti-tank guns which covered them, few as they were, put up a tenacious resistance.

After sustaining dreadful losses 9th Armoured Brigade broke the German anti-tank screen and 1st Armoured Division roared through, only to embroil itself in a major tank battle at a spot known as Tell El Aqqaqir. This brought the British advance to a temporary halt which enabled Rommel to begin his planned withdrawal to Fuka. At this crucial moment Hitler chose to intervene in the North African campaign for the first time. Invoking the support of the Italian High Command he ordered Rommel to stand and fight where he was, and Rommel obeyed. It was a gift to Montgomery. If the enemy had got back to Fuka and dug in it would have meant another Alamein. As it was the Allies launched a fresh attack on 3 December. This was fiercely resisted and soon became bogged down but overnight 5th Indian Brigade, with tank support and a devastating barrage, fortuitously struck the point where the German and Italian forces rubbed shoulders and broke through, almost without a fight. It was the breakthrough that Montgomery needed although it was too far south to pose an immediate threat to the bulk of Rommel's army up near the coast. This effectively ended the Battle of El Alamein and it is worth noting that, from published returns, the balance of tanks at this time stood at around 600 for the Allies, nearly 100 with the Italians and just 20 to the Germans.

In the meantime Rommel had received permission from the Führer to act on his own responsibility and he immediately ordered a withdrawal. It was not, however, to be a precipitate one. As the British armoured forces were released and directed north, to cut off the retreating enemy, they continually had to deal with a small but potent anti-tank screen, covered by the surviving Axis tanks, which slowed progress to a crawl.

Rommel's retreat to Fuka began on the night of 4 November. It was a night made bright by flares dropped by the RAF as they maintained a round-the-clock bombardment on the retreating enemy. Rommel's plan was to pull his mobile forces back to Fuka and hold it as far as he was able while the mass of German and Italian infantry was pulled out. The main problem he faced was transport, or rather the lack of it, and to compound it a desperate shortage of fuel. Those Axis forces to the south that had borne the brunt of Montgomery's final breakthrough were in a worse state. Those with transport at least had a chance but for the marching infantry capture was almost inevitable.

The British also had fuel problems. During the planning stage Brigadier Raymond Briggs had advised that one British armoured division be provided with an extra ration of fuel so that, when the breakthrough came, it could make a long-distance strike, at least as far as Sollum, to cut off any chance Rommel might have of retreat. However in the buildup to the battle all available transport had been committed to supplying ammunition so that, when the breakout came, objectives had to be limited and the turn north to the coast road executed considerably earlier than Briggs had advocated. Thus it was that, although a large British force was already across Rommel's line of retreat, most of his mobile units managed to slip through during the night and the position at Fuka was secured, at least for a while.

Even so, by the following afternoon it was clearly time to move on. The RAF continued to punish the Fuka position and Rommel's reconnaissance units reported increasing numbers of British tanks to the south. He was left with no alternative but to order a further withdrawal to Mersah Matruh and was quite unable to comply with instructions from Mussolini that his first duty was to extract the infantry. The road to Mersah was already packed with traffic. Every vehicle that could move was loaded with men but they were jammed, nose to tail, along the road. Those who tried to move around the jam by driving into the desert soon became bogged down and more effort was required to haul them out again. The RAF maintained continual pressure with bombing raids and low-flying attacks on this mass of transport. If all this was not bad enough the fuel situation was frustrating. Some 5,000 tons had been landed at Benghazi, the largest single quantity, according to Rommel, he had ever received, but that was at Benghazi and the tanks that desperately needed it were still east of Mersah Matruh. The distance was one problem, the RAF another, but of course once the precious liquid got anywhere near the fighting zone it became snarled up in the gigantic traffic jam striving to move west.

For the surviving German armour it was one long, running fight. The only advantage they had was that they could keep going at night whereas the British tanks generally halted when it got dark. There were reasons for such caution – uncharted minefields, potential enemy ambushes and the dreadful possibility of friendly fire incidents – but there is no doubt that the underlying cause of all this wariness was Rommel's reputation. His tendency to pull off a riposte when apparently devoid of resources had been underestimated so many times that nobody wanted to make the same mistake again. Even so 21st Panzer Division, or what was left of it, was halted through lack of fuel on 6 November when it was cornered by 22nd Armoured Brigade. The surviving German tanks formed a hedgehog around their transport and managed to hold out until it got dark. Enough fuel was brought in to get the wheeled transport moving but this famous unit was obliged to abandon its last fifteen tanks.

Then it began to rain. All night it poured down, especially along the coast. Rommel hardly saw this as a Godsend because any traffic not actually on the road became bogged down, but it was actually worse for the pursuers. Although tracked vehicles could keep going, the wheeled transport upon which they relied for resupplies of fuel and ammunition, not to mention food and other necessities, was immobilized. The situation on the morning of 7 November was such as to convince Montgomery that he could not trap Rommel and he reorganized his forces with a long pursuit in view. The New Zealand Division, with armour in support, fought its way along the coast road while, on the escarpment above, 7th Armoured Division began an outflanking move which was first directed to the Libyan frontier and then on to Tobruk.

On 8 November Rommel received further bad news. Axis intelligence reported an Allied convoy of 104 ships apparently making for the North African coast and it soon became clear that landings were taking place in the west. To quote Rommel *this spelt the end of the Army in Africa.* From now on it was simply a calendar of retreats. The Germans reached the old Gazala position on 11 November, where more huge traffic jams occurred. They abandoned Tobruk the following day and on 13 November the leading elements reached Mersa Brega again. Although tempted to try Wavell's trick of cutting off the retreating enemy Montgomery remained cautious. He would always consolidate supplies before moving and clearly intended to keep the main body of Rommel's army in constant view to prevent him from doing anything unexpected. Even so, some armoured cars were despatched along the direct route through Msus and, although they were held up for some time by the rain, their presence was enough to worry Rommel.

As if he did not have enough troubles the German commander now discovered that ammunition, fuel and water supplies upon which he was relying were often being destroyed by over-zealous quartermasters before he could use them. Although ordered to hold the Mersa Brega line, which was already occupied by Italian infantry and an armoured division, Rommel pointed out that it would inevitably be outflanked and the non-motorized Italian infantry would simply be sacrificed again. However the opposition to

further retreat was so strong that Rommel was eventually obliged to fly to Europe to present his own point of view.

That he was not successful may be judged by the repeated orders to *resist to the uttermost* issued by Mussolini who, in the same breath, instructed Rommel to save Italian troops, even at the expense of the Germans. While this discussion was taking place, British armour was moving west, below the horizon to the south. Rommel prepared a defence line further west at Buerat, which he knew could not be held, while the Italians had their own based on Homs to cover Tripoli. However, on 23 January 1943 British armour rolled into Tripoli.

The start of El Alamein. Shermans of 2nd Armoured Brigade move towards a horizon made bright by the massive artillery barrage. Conceived on First World War proportions the general barrage of over 1,000 guns was staged at maximum intensity for fifteen minutes and then switched to selective targets when the infantry went in. It was the shock from a near miss that caused General Stumme's heart attack, while shortage of ammunition limited the Germans' power to reply in kind.

Italian M13/40 tanks advancing. Unlike the Germans, who upgraded the armour and armament of their tanks at regular intervals, the Italians never fielded anything more powerful than this through the entire desert campaign. New designs were being prepared in Italy but none ever progressed beyond the prototype stage. However gallantly they were handled there was no way that these machines could stand up to the newer American tanks for very long.

RTR crews preparing their Shermans for action. These are of the welded M4A2 type (Sherman IIIs to the British) powered by twin General Motors diesel engines. Each tank carried a mixture of armour-piercing, high-explosive and smoke rounds for the 75-mm gun and in addition had a co-axial Browning machine-gun in the turret and another in the front of the hull, operated by the co-driver.

Another result of the Lend-Lease Act was a supply of M7, 105-mm self-propelled guns from America. Nicknamed 'Priests' by the Royal Artillery they used the engine, transmission and suspension of the M3 Medium tank. They were lightly armoured, and devoid of any overhead protection but would not be expected to operate in the front line with the tanks.

With the Matildas now relegated to support roles the brunt of the initial attacks was borne by Valentines. Here an RTR crewman from *Cheetah* chats with a couple of RAF officers. The contribution to Alamein made by the RAF and its Commonwealth counterparts was massive and became even more significant during the ensuing pursuit.

Six of the new Churchill infantry tanks took part in the Alamein battle, their first action since the unfortunate landing at Dieppe. The Churchill Mark III carried a 6-pdr gun in a welded turret and the frontal armour was an impressive 102 mm thick. Commanded by an officer of the Royal Gloucestershire Hussars, Major Norris King, the tanks operated as Kingforce. One was knocked out in the battle but the remainder fought again at Tel el Aqqaqir.

Another view of a dug-in 88-mm, now abandoned. Even at a range of 2,000 yd these guns could penetrate 84 mm of armour, which meant every type of Allied tank except the Churchill was vulnerable. Digging these big guns in required considerable effort but British tank crews claimed that they could only spot them when they elevated to deal with enemy aircraft.

An interesting example of German innovation, captured during the Alamein battle. Based on a Bussing-NAG 5-ton half-track this combination, known as *Diana*, mounted a captured Russian 7.62-cm field gun within a large armoured box. Nine of them were operated by the 605th Panzerjägerabteilung and they were first encountered by British troops during the Gazala battle.

The problem of the minefields. This photograph, which according to the original caption, was of a trial, shows the effect of an anti-tank mine on a Daimler Dingo scout car. The casualties, presumably dummies, have been thrown clear of the vehicle, the front end of which has been entirely destroyed. Minefields were used to create impassable areas in an otherwise featureless landscape but they were a double-edged weapon.

Armoured Command Vehicles, based on AEC Matador artillery tractors, were a form of mobile office, map room and communications centre for divisional and other senior commanders. Britain was the only country to produce anything quite so specialized and they were very popular. Rommel used a captured one, nicknamed *Mammuth*, of which he was very proud. It even features in letters to his wife.

A general view of the battlefield during the breakthrough after Alamein, here in the New Zealand sector. The original caption claims that the smoke is coming from burning German Panzer III tanks while the transport in the middle distance is definitely British. More smoke can be seen miles away, on the distant horizon, demonstrating the amazing vistas that greeted desert travellers. There would be nowhere at all to hide under air attack.

Sherman and Crusader tanks spread out over the desert following the final breakthrough of Rommel's defences. Many British armoured regiments at this time had two squadrons of Crusaders and one of Shermans or Grants. Over the following months, as more American tanks arrived, the proportion changed so that by December each regiment had just one squadron of Crusaders.

A Sherman of C Squadron, the Queen's Bays in Mersah Matruh. Many of these crews had been driving and fighting continually for nearly four days and were completely exhausted. Notice how, in true Eighth Army fashion, the Bays have already decorated their new tanks with all the paraphernalia required to live comfortably in the desert. A selection of packs dangle from the side rails and there are other items stowed on the track guards and engine deck.

A British signaller tests his line, sheltering by the wreck of a disabled Panzer III as a Stuart races by. Although in many respects the equal of contemporary British cruiser tanks the Stuart soon came to be regarded as a light tank, probably on account of its lively performance, and was employed by the reconnaissance troops of armoured divisions. The advantage of the Panzer III was that it could, and did, take a larger gun and thicker armour to keep pace with battlefield requirements.

Irrepressible Jocks. The crew of a Universal Carrier and their friends raise a cheer for the camera. Powered by a Ford V8 engine and employing a curious steering system that curved the tracks by adjusting the suspension. Carriers were as easy to drive as a truck, if not quite so comfortable. They were employed by nearly every branch of the British and Commonwealth armies for every purpose imaginable but the protection they afforded was minimal and steel helmets were essential.

It was during the Tel el Aqqaqir battle that a reconnaissance troop from 10th Royal Hussars, inspecting some wrecked German tanks, captured the German General Ritter von Thoma, who was commanding the counter-attack of 21st Panzer and 90th Light Divisions. He is seen here dismounting from the Scout Car of Captain Grant Singer. This young officer was killed a day or so later when his troop ran into an 88-mm battery.

Transport of the New Zealand Division, escorted by a Stuart tank, moving through the ruins of Sollum in November. The New Zealand 2nd Infantry Division gained a remarkable reputation for itself in the Western Desert. Stuarts were operated by the 2nd Division Cavalry Regiment and the New Zealanders later created an armoured brigade, equipped with Shermans, which fought with great distinction in the Italian campaign.

The officer in the RTR beret, standing at the right of this group, is General Raymond Briggs commanding 1st Armoured Division. It was Briggs who tried to persuade Montgomery to keep an armoured division up his sleeve to exploit the breakthrough when Rommel retreated. It seems that he is not just posing alongside the wrecked Crusader on the right. A signaller can be seen sitting beside the tank – which appears to have been mined – and the cables from his headset seem to lead into the wrecked tank so they may well be using its wireless set.

The Germans made considerable use of self-propelled anti-aircraft guns to protect mobile units. In this case the carrier vehicle is a 1-ton SdKfz 10 half-track built by Demag, mounting a 2-cm Flak gun. This photograph was taken after capture, with a British soldier sitting at the gun. Quite how effective these weapons were against aircraft is difficult to assess but the German Army had large numbers of them on a variety of chassis.

As Rommel's forces retreated from the El Alamein position the shortage of fuel began to take its toll. Under constant pressure from land and air, units scattered and fought isolated rearguard actions. If they could not get away tanks were often sacrificed to cover the retreat of Axis infantry and transport. Here two Panzer IIIs and a Panzer IV Special lie abandoned in the desert.

Then came the rain. A Grant tank of the Staffordshire Yeomanry leads a transport column down a flooded road en route for Mersah Matruh. The rain began on the afternoon of 6 November and the historian of the Staffordshire Yeomanry claims that it was impossible to operate away from the main roads, which caused a great deal of congestion. The 10th Hussars blamed the rain for delaying the delivery of much-needed fuel supplies and there is no doubt that it afforded Rommel some relief and respite from air attacks.

A column of captured enemy infantry escorted by a couple of Humber armoured cars. Some regimental histories, written just after the war, accuse Rommel of abandoning the Italian troops to their fate. In fact, as Rommel himself makes clear, there was simply insufficient transport to extricate such troops and German infantry went into the bag as well. In any case, now that the landings in Tunisia had taken place, there were many ready to acknowledge, with Rommel, that it was the end for Axis aspirations in Africa.

Stuart tanks passing the cathedral in Benghazi in December 1942. This must have been at least the fifth time that the town had changed hands during the war and the Italian colonists might be forgiven for treating both sides equally as liberators in their turn. For all that, in this view at any rate, it seems to have remained largely untouched by the ravages of war and must have been a pleasant haven of civilization for both sides after months in the desert.

Armoured cars of Eighth Army leading the advance on Tripoli. The leading car is a Humber with a Marmon-Herrington behind it. The exploits of the armoured cars are continually overshadowed by those of the tanks but they had an exciting war and the desert increased their scope considerably. Most British vehicles operated on Runflat tyres, which would hold up for 20 miles or more after being punctured. Even so a spare was normally carried.

Valentines of 40th RTR entering Tripoli on 23 January 1943, the first British tanks to reach the city. The 40th had been awarded the unofficial title 'Monty's Foxhounds' by the infantry because they had been in the van of virtually every attack since Alamein. Rommel, by this time, was organizing his troops on the Mareth Line and it is interesting to note that, unlike the situation elsewhere, the Germans appear to have made no attempt to plant booby traps or mines in the city itself, no doubt out of consideration for the civilian population.

CHAPTER 6
OPERATION TORCH

The news which so upset Rommel on 8 November 1942, concerning the Anglo-American landings in the west, was not the result of a snap decision based on the outcome of Alamein. In fact the Allied plan was agreed in July 1942 and confirmed on 15 September 1942. The decision probably had more to do with events in Russia than in Egypt and indeed political considerations seem to have had more bearing on Operation Torch than any other factors. It is interesting to observe that, although the landings were on a tiny scale compared with D-Day in Normandy, or even most of those in Sicily and Italy, and the opposition to be expected was not so great, it was probably one of the most distant invasions of all. Troops sailed direct from Britain and the United States to land in Algeria or French Morocco. It meant that the attacking forces had to cover thousands of sea miles infested with enemy U-boats. Not only that, Allied naval and air forces had to control most of the western Mediterranean while the landings were taking place and during the planning stage there were no guarantees that most of the airfields in Libya would not be in Axis hands.

The operation was under the overall command of General Dwight D. Eisenhower and it was launched as a three-pronged attack. In each case the landing centred on a major city port: Casablanca in the west, Oran at the centre and Algiers to the east. The tragedy was that in each case the opposition was not German or Italian but an erstwhile ally, France – or at least that part of France controlled by the Vichy government. The tactic employed in each case was the same, namely to pinch out the respective cities by landings on either side; in the case of Oran and Algiers, a limited amount of direct assault was also involved.

The western task force, which had sailed direct from the United States, was commanded by Major General George S. Patton. It met with considerable resistance which took three days to subdue, but Casablanca was in American hands by 11 November. The central task force, which was an all-American operation mounted from the United Kingdom, included an airborne element. It also encountered some tough opposition but had it all under control by 10 November.

At Algiers, apart from an attempt to take the port by direct action, which resulted in the loss of the destroyer HMS *Broke*, things went relatively well. The Algiers landing, a combined Anglo-American affair, benefited from a certain amount of subterfuge that resulted in a pro-Allied faction controlling most of the defences. It was secured by the night of 8 November.

The tank forces committed to Eisenhower's command were 1st and 2nd Armored Divisions of the United States Army and British 6th Armoured Division. This last was equipped entirely with Crusader and Valentine tanks while the Americans employed M3 Lee, M4 Sherman and M3 or M5 Stuart tanks. The Americans also fielded tank destroyer battalions, whose role was self-explanatory. At this stage of the war these were mainly equipped with lightly armoured half-tracks, mounting 75-mm guns.

The key to this new campaign was clearly Tunis itself, for with Tunis taken the Axis forces would be cut off from Europe and their supplies would soon run out. Tunisia would be in Allied hands and Rommel would have nowhere to go. The French were at best an ambivalent enemy and there was no obvious reason why a rapidly moving force should not take the city swiftly. In order to achieve this a special formation, known as Blade Force, was created. It consisted of an armoured car squadron of 1st Derbyshire Yeomanry, the tanks of 17/21st Lancers and an American light tank battalion, with a full complement of supporting arms, infantry, artillery and engineers. Blade Force left

Algiers on 15 November and dashed east, covering some 200 miles in forty-eight hours, but by then Hitler had made his move. Uncertain as to French attitudes he, along with Mussolini, ordered the occupation of Vichy France and Corsica while two Panzer divisions and one infantry division were rushed across to Tunisia from France. Now, with defeat the only realistic outcome, the German dictator was willing to release troops that were earlier denied to Rommel when victory was in sight.

Blade Force got remarkably close to Tunis, and the American element distinguished itself by an impromptu raid on an enemy airfield, but it was held up in the foothills by tough German and Italian resistance and suffered heavily, as did the US 1st Armored Division on its right. The Americans have often been criticized for their inexperience at this time but in terms of actual combat the regiments of British 6th Armoured Division were in exactly the same state. Even so both divisions fought some very effective actions against battle-hardened opponents and in many cases it was 57-mm guns in Crusaders and Valentines or 37-mm guns in Stuarts being employed against the long 75-mm guns of late pattern Panzer IVs.

Through the remainder of November and December the Allies made repeated efforts to capture Tunis but future plans were now dependent on Montgomery and, since he was not expected to cross the Tunisian frontier before February, Eisenhower's more ambitious plans were shelved. Meanwhile the new German commander, General von Arnim, launched a series of attacks westwards into the Atlas foothills, most of which seem to have been directed against the French; they were generally successful. By January 1943 Blade Force had been disbanded and 17/21st Lancers were at a location in the hills called Bou Arada, facing north to confront German forces covering Tunis. The regiment had received three M3 Medium tanks from the Americans, two of which were destroyed shortly afterwards. In an attack against French forces at Robaa at the end of January, the Germans employed a dozen tanks of which at least two were Panzer VI Tigers. These huge tanks were ambushed by a British anti-tank battery and knocked out; one was recovered by the Germans but the other had to be blown up after the 17/21st failed to tow it away.

The most serious test of American armour came on 14 February 1943 at a location called Kasserine Pass in southern Tunisia. By this time, of course, Rommel had pulled out of Tripolitania and created a strong defensive position at Mareth but for all practical purposes his forces and those of von Arnim could be considered to have combined. However, the two men did not see eye to eye and this spoiled their chances at Kasserine; their lack of success was no credit to the Allied command which was in a worse state of confusion. The battle itself was complex. It was fought through a maze of valleys which led out of the central pass between Sidi Bou Zid and Kasserine and it began with a two-pronged attack by 10th and 21st Panzer Divisions

(under von Arnim) heading west into the pass and the Deutsche Afrika Korps (now an Italo-German force under Rommel) driving up a subsidiary pass from the south.

The mass of von Arnim's armour, rolling in from the east preceded by waves of dive-bombers, hit the Americans very hard and 1st Armored Division's counter-attack on 15 February was an unmitigated disaster. The American column advanced down the valley with tanks to the front, armoured infantry behind and tank destroyers on either flank. Their objective was Sidi Bou Zid but the hills on either side were in German hands – comparison with the Charge of the Light Brigade would not be inappropriate. The Germans held their fire to begin with but the Americans soon found it difficult to maintain their formation. The pass was crossed at various points by deep wadis, or dried-up stream beds, which tanks could only get over at selected spots. Thus the approach to each wadi first involved a fair amount of searching to find the crossing place, followed by a concentration of vehicles as they filed over. Once through they could fan out again, until they arrived at the next wadi. It was on these wadis that the Germans concentrated their fire. The result proved that courage itself was no substitute for experience and when the Allies regained the pass a month later they discovered the burnt-out hulks of some forty tanks scattered across the battlefield.

Despite this success the Germans were unable to derive any permanent advantage from it. Their forces penetrated a number of valleys in the area but they were hampered by the split command. Rommel wanted to head straight for the town of Tedessa, a move which he believed would cause the Allies to withdraw, but von Arnim refused to cooperate. Rommel attempted to get his way by going over von Arnim's head to Field Marshal Kesselring and he got a favourable reply, only to have it modified by the Italians who, for some reason, insisted he go through adjacent valleys which led to the small settlements of Thala and Sbiba. At these locations they were attacked and stopped by the three reunited tank regiments of 26th Armoured Brigade in British 6th Armoured Division. The brigade had been in the process of converting from its mixed establishment of Crusaders and Valentines to Shermans when the emergency at Kasserine erupted and to their dismay the men had to go back to their old tanks for this desperate action.

At first, of course, it was impossible to guess which way the German thrust would go and there was a good deal of switching from one valley to the next and a fair bit of getting lost, but when the fighting began it worked out roughly that 16/5th Lancers were at Sbiba with 17/21st Lancers and 2nd Lothian & Border Horse at Thala, the latter with a detached squadron out in front charged with delaying the Germans for as long as possible. They did this magnificently, against 10th Panzer Division guided by Rommel himself, but at the cost of all eleven of their Valentines and their squadron leader. In fact this was very much a battle for the Valentines, most of which were still armed with the old 2-pdr gun. More than one regimental history explains that the majority of Crusaders had been abandoned after breakdowns so the regiments were even denied the slight advantage of their 6-pdrs. There were instances of Valentines knocking out Panzer IVs but they are rare. Invariably the British tanks came under effective fire long before they were able to fight back and it was a question of hanging on to the existing ridge for as long as one dared and then falling back, under fire, to start the whole process over again with whatever tanks were left. The German tanks were supplemented by large numbers of self-propelled guns. Rommel claims that he had asked von Arnim for some of the nineteen Tiger tanks to beef up this attack but that von Arnim had refused on the grounds that they were all under repair. Discovering later that this was untrue, Rommel made the obvious deduction that von Arnim wanted to keep them all for himself.

On the other side of the valley 17/21st Lancers were down to a dozen tanks by dusk of the same day and they had just withdrawn from their forward positions when more tanks were heard coming down the road. Soon a Valentine appeared through the murk and the obvious conclusion was reached that it was a straggler coming home. In fact it was in German hands and leading a column of enemy tanks. Their appearance resulted in a short-range fire fight which cost the Germans seven tanks and prevented their breakthrough. Even so it was a close-run thing and the Germans had not given up entirely. Yet the two British regiments between them could hardly muster enough tanks to create one respectable squadron and their infantry was also suffering badly. It was thus with some relief that the following evening tanks were heard coming up from the rear which turned out to be the 16/5th, now released from their position at Sbiba. What is more, the regiment now had nineteen of its Shermans in the line, leading the way. With American and British infantry in support they went forward to new positions, only to discover that the enemy had gone.

Landing Craft Assault (LCA) waiting to pick up troops from a transport during the landings at Oran. Further inshore a destroyer creates a smoke screen around another large transport to shield it from coast defence batteries onshore. Those enemy guns that did open fire were immediately engaged by Allied warships, and some Vichy French destroyers that tried to escape were sunk. In fact the main risk to shipping came from U-boats and, on the beaches further east, air attacks.

Landings on the beaches around Algiers were such mild affairs that the local population came out to watch. Here a half-track gun motor carriage, mounting a 75-mm howitzer, is seen on the beach, possibly with a spot of engine trouble. This must have been one of the first occasions when the famous Allied five-pointed white star was seen in a theatre of war.

The Vichy French forces that were available to oppose the Allied landings were poorly equipped. In this case a soldier inspects a French armoured car, the design of which goes back to the First World War. It is a White Laffly, a 1918 model rebuilt onto a more modern chassis in 1932. The turret mounts a 37-mm cannon, in this case facing to the rear, with an 8-mm Hotchkiss machine-gun in the opposite face of the turret. By 1942 standards it was woefully out of date.

It was deemed important to give the French the idea that the invasion force was American, in order to avoid other political complications. Thus many of the vehicles were marked quite dramatically with the American flag, as shown on this M4A1 Sherman. The French officer in the hull gunner's seat and the young man in the turret suggest that a bit of international bridge building is going on.

Another American half-track, shortly after landing. It is also adorned with Old Glory and the way the exhaust pipe is continued up the side of the body shows that it was prepared for deep wading, a practice still in its infancy. These lightly armoured vehicles were built by a variety of firms including White, International and Diamond T. As a personnel carrier the M2 version carried ten men and had a top speed of 40 mph. Unlike the German machines these American half-tracks had driven front axles and reinforced rubber tracks.

When Blade Force set out for Tunis it was led by 56th Reconnaissance Regiment which was equipped with Humber Light Reconnaissance Cars. The example shown here is not part of that force but a sample car apparently under test by the Egyptian branch of the Mechanisation Experimental Establishment (MEE) which had its headquarters at Chertsey in Surrey. The MEE examined all new military types and a branch in the Middle East was a natural offshoot. The other vehicle is also a Humber, a four-wheel drive utility vehicle which carries the MEE badge on its door.

A Crusader IICS of 6th Armoured Division in Tunisia. CS stands for Close Support and indicates a tank fitted with a 3-in howitzer instead of the normal 2-pdr. Such tanks were issued to regimental and squadron headquarters with the main purpose of firing smoke shells. High-explosive rounds were available but, for some reason, rarely used. It is also interesting to note that this particular tank has the Allied white star painted on the turret top, no doubt as an aid to recognition from the air.

American Stuart tanks operating with British infantry, probably on a training exercise. These are M3A1 Light Tank which had a new-style turret, without a commander's cupola but now featuring a rotating turret basket in the fighting compartment. The white band, painted midway round the turret, was also seen on American tanks training in the USA and Britain but it was soon dropped.

One of the most unusual combat vehicles fielded by the US Army was the Gun Motor Carriage M6. It was nothing more than a Dodge ¾-ton, four-wheel drive truck with a 37-mm anti-tank gun mounted at the back. As a vehicle intended to fight tanks it was about as practical as the British 2-pdr portee. In an ambush position, as here among the Tunisian cactus, it might have one chance, but it would not get a second.

A more practical design for a tank destroyer was the 75-mm Gun Motor Carriage M3, which at least had a decent gun, mounted on an armoured half-track chassis. Like the previous vehicle the crew have adopted a local camouflage by smearing mud over the basic olive drab paint. The main gun fires forwards over the bonnet, but here another crew member with a .50 calibre Browning keeps watch for enemy aircraft.

The first news Allied military intelligence had of the presence of Tiger tanks in Tunisia was this photograph, which appeared in the *Nationale Zeitung* of 11 December 1942. It shows a Tiger, running on its narrow transport tracks, rolling through the streets of Tunis shortly after landing, having been shipped from Reggio in southern Italy. The huge tank must have made quite an impression on the crowd. It is seen here without the prominent muzzle brake, normally fitted to the 88-mm gun.

One of the two Tigers knocked out by British 6-pdrs on the Robaa road, 20 January 1943. An internal fire has burned much of the paint off the turret but otherwise the tank is quite intact. That night the Germans managed to recover the other Tiger, leaving the Panzer III seen in the distance. British experts were on the way to study the Tiger but attempts by 17/21st Lancers to tow it away were not successful.

Faced with the prospect of losing this second tank the Royal Engineers decided to blow it up, with the result shown here. The experts, when they arrived, selected sample chunks of armour to be sent back to Britain for evaluation. The length of track in the foreground came from the 6th Armoured Division Valentine on the left. It is reported to have run over a mine while trying to get by the disabled Tiger.

The Panzer III seen on the road behind the Tiger (opposite) was of the Ausf. N type, introduced in 1942. It mounted the short 75-mm gun originally fitted to the Panzer IV. These tanks were attached to the heavy Tiger battalions to give the big tanks close support against infantry attacks. The short 75-mm was able to fire an effective high-explosive round at short range, which was impossible for the Tiger's 88-mm to achieve.

A mixed American column, all liberally coated with the Tunisian mud camouflage. A half-track leads, followed by the American version of the M3 Medium tank, known to British troops as the General Lee, and an M3A1 light tank brings up the rear. The Lee's turret was different in style from that of the Grant, with a separate rotating cupola for the commander which was, in effect, a tiny machine-gun turret in its own right.

From about 1936 the Germans started to develop an impressive range of eight-wheeled armoured cars which proved particularly useful in desert conditions. The basic model, the SdKfz 231, was equipped with a turret-mounted 2-cm cannon and MG34 machine-gun and had a top speed of 50 mph. This example, captured in Tunisia, is being shown to a group of British war correspondents.

Of all the armoured regiments, British or American, that fought in Tunisia, few earned a reputation to compare with the 1st Derbyshire Yeomanry, ostensibly the divisional armoured car regiment of 6th Armoured Division. The Americans, with whom they worked regularly, had nothing but praise once they got used to their austere British ways. Here a troop from A Squadron, consisting of a Daimler armoured car and Daimler Dingo scout car, pose for the camera.

The Tunisian campaign was the first in which American, British and German parachute forces were deployed. Having up to that time painted German paratroops as little better than saboteurs or spies, the British were naturally now keen to show that their own airborne troops were heroes. Even so, there is no doubt that the Germans were superbly equipped, even down to specialist air-portable vehicles such as the tiny NSU Kettenrad, a sort of half-tracked motorcycle. Some were operational in Tunisia where this one was captured after being burned out.

Two M3 Lee medium tanks with an M3 Stuart light tank between them of 1st Armored Division. Nicknamed 'Old Ironsides', 1st Armored was raised at Fort Knox, Kentucky, in July 1940. Commanded in Tunisia by Major General Orlando Ward the division later passed to Major General Lucien Truscott who commanded it in Italy. Tunisia was the only combat zone in which American troops used their M3 medium tank and it does not seem to have been accepted with the same enthusiasm displayed by the British.

An M4A1 Sherman towing a half-track through a wadi at Sidi-Bou-Zid, at the eastern end of the Kasserine Pass. The nature of a typical wadi, which in many places could not be crossed by any vehicle because of its high walls, is clearly shown here, illustrating how the Americans were forced to group their tanks in order to get across, thereby providing the German gunners with a mass of targets.

Another Panzer IV Special clearly knocked out but still largely intact. Comparing the performance of the American and German 75-mm guns one finds that the weapon in the Sherman could penetrate 40 mm of armour at 2,000 yd while the German gun, firing comparable ammunition at the same range, would go through 53 mm. Since the Panzer IV Ausf. F2 and M4A1 Sherman had frontal hull armour of 50 mm, the result, at least on paper, was a foregone conclusion.

Crusader III tanks of 6th Armoured Division in a defensive leaguer on the Tunisian uplands. Although it was in no way comparable to the Sherman, let alone the Panzer IV, the British tank was used with considerable gallantry by the three regiments of the division. Unlike their counterparts from the desert the men of 6th Armoured Division, whose tanks were painted dark green, never acquired the Eighth Army habit of cluttering up their vehicles with that delightful jumble of external stowage that characterized the desert veterans.

Cleaning the 6-pdr gun of a Crusader III on a mountain track. Despite the fact that 6th Armoured Division's tanks had come directly from Britain and might be supposed to have been in better shape than those of Eighth Army, the regimental histories make it quite clear that they still suffered from serious defects which kept most of them out of action. One can understand why the men were so eager to get hold of Shermans.

The original, official caption claims that these vehicles were mounting a surprise attack which drove the Axis forces from their positions. It is probably an inflated claim. The two half-tracks, one carrying a 105-mm howitzer, the other a heavy Browning machine-gun, could well be providing fire support for an attack, but it would take more firepower than this to discomfort hardened Axis troops.

Here American troops appear to be making sensible use of a wadi. The Sherman tank has selected a hull-down position below the edge of the crest, where its turret is the only thing visible to the enemy, while the infantry half-tracks and a cluster of Jeeps shelter beneath the ridge. Whether the figures standing on the skyline would be there if this was a genuine action photograph is another matter. Common sense suggests probably not.

CHAPTER 7
TANKS IN THE HILLS

The pursuit westwards from Tripoli was entrusted to 7th Armoured Division which, in tank terms, consisted of 40th RTR supplemented by C Squadron of 50th RTR. Progress was hindered by mines, demolitions and, in particular, various forms of ingenious booby trap which the Germans had developed into a sort of art form.

Following the events at Kasserine Pass Rommel returned to attack his old opponent, the Eighth Army, which was now focusing its strength on the Mareth Line. The Axis attack, executed by the Italian General Messe, might have been successful had not 22nd Armoured Brigade managed to establish itself in the Tadjera Hills. From the Allied point of view the Battle of Medenine, fought on 6 March 1943, was primarily an anti-tank battle. Elements of 10th, 15th and 21st Panzer Divisions along with 90th Light and the Italian Spezia Divisions battered themselves against well-sited anti-tank batteries, supported in some cases by 3.7-in anti-aircraft guns, in an effort to break through to the key crossroads at Medenine. In the meantime Rommel had

returned to Europe for medical treatment. He was destined not to return to North Africa but this information was suppressed by Berlin; Rommel's reputation was still a considerable threat in itself.

The Mareth Line, which blocked the route west between the Matmata Hills and the sea, was regarded by the British High Command as an obstacle to equal the German positions at El Alamein and plans were laid to deal with it accordingly. At its northern end the line was enhanced by the Wadi Zigzaou, which was not entirely dry at this time of year. Crossing points were to be created by Valentine tanks of 50th RTR dropping fascines (bundles of sticks) just as their forbears had done at Cambrai in the First World War. The causeway thus created held up well enough under the relatively light weight of the Valentines but their tracks tore the fascines to shreds so that wheeled tractors, with anti-tank guns, were unable to cross. Neither could the Shermans of 22nd Armoured Brigade since they were too heavy.

Thus it was that 50th RTR, supported by one or two anti-tank guns which did get over the Wadi, spent a heartbreaking day and night fending off persistent attacks by 15th Panzer Division which, in due course, drove the few surviving Valentines back to the Wadi. Two days were spent trying to consolidate the crossings since this was intended to be the spearhead of the main attack but in the end it failed. Fortunately, in an endeavour to deceive his opponents, Montgomery had also despatched the 2nd New Zealand Division on a wide outflanking march aimed at El Hamma and the Gabes Gap to the rear of the Mareth position. This was now reinforced by 1st Armoured Division which drove through the New Zealanders as they began their attack and, in a protective formation, drove on to the El Hamma position during the night. This created a fair amount of havoc which even resulted in the padre of 9th Lancers capturing a battery of 88-mm anti-aircraft guns by mistake. More importantly this incursion from the south prompted the evacuation of the Mareth Line. The enemy held Gabes, on the coast road, long enough to cover their retreat from Mareth and now moved into position on the Wadi Akarit, just beyond Gabes.

Returning now to the First Army in central Tunisia shortly after the fighting in and around Kasserine Pass we find von Arnim planning a new offensive against the town of Beja, a major communications centre. The original German plan was to mount a series of raids from the north against advanced Allied positions and to exploit the most successful with an all-out attack. However, von Arnim, believing the

battle at Kasserine to have been more effective than in fact it was, launched straight into the main attack. From the tank point of view the highlight was the assault on Hunt's Gap, a narrow defile in mountainous country on the direct route to Beja.

The German attack was led by a mixed force of seventy-four tanks that included twelve Panzer IV Specials and fourteen Tigers, but its commander, Colonel Rudolph Lang, was directed through the mountains, which restricted his ability to use his armour effectively. Hunt's Gap was screened by a battalion of the Hampshire regiment with supporting artillery, covered further back by more artillery and a tank regiment, the North Irish Horse. The NIH were in Churchill tanks, one of six regiments of Churchills recently despatched to Tunisia following the modest success of Kingforce at El Alamein. Lang's force smashed through the screen on 26 February but the defenders of Hunt's Gap held him and when it was all over Lang had just seven tanks left. This was mainly down to the effective cooperation of artillery and tanks in the defence and some treacherous ground, but also to the practice of sending sappers onto the battlefield after each attack to destroy any disabled German tanks which might otherwise be recovered. Lang himself was awarded the nickname 'Tank Killer' by his own men but it was not intended as a compliment.

South of Hunt's Gap another arm of von Arnim's offensive was aimed at El Aroussa, a vital road junction, and the

British defence force here included A Squadron, 51st RTR, another Churchill regiment. On 28 February the tanks were ordered to investigate German positions at a location known as Steamroller Farm where they were treated to a heavy air attack and a number of Churchills were knocked out by anti-tank guns. The squadron commander, Major Hadfield, ordered his No. 1 Troop to break through but by this time the troop consisted of just one tank, commanded by Captain E.D. Hollands. Even so Hollands rushed the farm and headed for the hills beyond, knocking out two 88-mm guns on the way. The Churchill then swung off the road and started uphill and it was here that the slow, heavy tank revealed an unbelievable ability to climb. Reaching the top Hollands spotted an enemy transport column waiting on the road below and he set about wrecking it. Joined by another Churchill Hollands then destroyed a pair of German tanks before retiring.

The Germans clearly did not realize that there was nothing more to prevent them from advancing. They had lost virtually all their supporting transport and the entire attack was called off. German reports speak of a 'mad British tank battalion' which 'scaled impossible heights'. This was true to the extent that such climbing was beyond the power of most tanks, but not the Churchill.

The attack on the Mareth Line was to be assisted by a move against German positions further north by US II Corps. Following the Kasserine battle it was felt that the Americans should not be committed to anything too intense so their role was seen as a threat rather than a major attack. At this time II Corps' commander, the eccentric Lloyd Fredenhall, was replaced by General Patton who had far more ambitious plans for his new command, plans that were only restrained with difficulty by General Eisenhower. The Americans would be returning to an area that they had fought over in February when 1st Armored Division had tried consequences with 21st Panzer Division and suffered as a result.

Following reconnaissance by 1st Derbyshire Yeomanry the Americans began a long drive south towards the vital road junction at Gafsa. Dreadful spring weather, torrential rain and hail, reduced the roads to a state which brought armour and transport to a halt but, after enemy outposts and mines were cleared, Gafsa was entered without opposition. Their next objective, Station de Sened, was outflanked and taken on 21 March and from there all that was required was a move east for about 20 miles to threaten Axis positions at Maknassy. However these plans were soon altered to include the capture of Maknassy and a nearby airfield and, despite general exhaustion among the leading troops, this was achieved on the following day.

Attempts to go further were frustrated by tanks losing their tracks on the rocky ground and by a gradual stiffening of resistance as the Germans, under the redoubtable 'Tank Killer' Lang, dug in. Failure to capture the enemy airfield meant that the Germans had air support immediately available and despite desperate urging from Patton the advance soon slowed down. Meanwhile the enemy, having recognized the purpose of this pincer movement towards the coast, started to bring up tanks. In conjunction with the attack on Maknassy US 1st Infantry Division was directed further south, through the settlement of El Guettar and on to some hills overlooking the Gabes road. This success soon drew a response from the Germans in the shape of 10th Panzer Division, which was beaten off, but a further attempt by the Americans to open the pass for an advance by 1st Armored Division failed.

The original plan, imposed on General Patton, had now been altered three times in response to events and now it was to be changed again. The new scheme was to create a mobile, armoured force – to be called Benson Force after its commander – which would move swiftly down the Gabes road and smash its way through with the infantry in its wake. Yet all the while German resistance was increasing, with 21st Panzer Division coming up to join the 10th. Although Montgomery had already got around the Mareth position it was every bit as important to keep a route open for retreat as it was to try to hold the Eighth Army at Wadi Akarit.

The Americans ran into 21st Panzer at El Guettar on 30 March and were thrown back. They tried again the next day. This was not successful either and every attempt the Americans made, both here and at

Maknassy, was subjected to fierce air attacks. The infantry took over again on 2 April and after four days fighting the Germans began to withdraw, followed by Benson Force.

Hitler pronounced that Wadi Akarit was to be the last line of defence in Tunisia, but that was easy to say in Berlin. At a conference between German and Italian commanders von Arnim countered the optimism of Field Marshal Kesselring by saying that in his view it was the British who would decide how long they held Wadi Akarit, not Hitler or Mussolini.

When it came the Eighth Army assault on Wadi Akarit was not as well organized as it might have been. There was an element of misunderstanding, to say the least, at Corps command level and the opportunity to finish off the defenders was again lost. Some lessons were learnt however. For instance when the Valentines of 50th RTR crossed the Wadi they were towing anti-tank guns and carrying their crews. Further inland the Indian troops distinguished themselves by capturing the high ground of the Djebel Tebaga Fatnassa but when the Staffordshire Yeomanry and 3rd RTR attempted to exploit this success they were blocked by a few well-sited 88-mm guns which had not been dealt with in the initial attacks.

Even so, by the evening of 7 April, those enemy forces that had not surrendered abandoned the Wadi Akarit line and were streaming across the coastal plain northwards, towards the next appointed defensive position at Enfidaville. An Allied attempt to cut them off using First Army troops supported by US 1st Armored Division and British 6th Armoured Division was foiled by stubborn German defence of the pass at Fondouk and misunderstanding between the Allies which resulted in some bad feeling. By the time the British and American armour broke out onto the coastal plain it was only to see the survivors of the Wadi Akarit battle heading away from them to the north. Twice, in a matter of days, the enemy had managed to slip through a well-prepared trap, just as they had done in every battle since El Alamein.

With Tripoli in British hands Montgomery's biggest problem, the long supply route back to Egypt, was solved. Here he was able to recruit his strength, bring in new equipment and build up a base that would support future operations. In this photograph a Liberty Ship, at anchor off the port, discharges into a couple of tank landing craft, in this case the LCT (2).

Among the new arrivals were some improved versions of the Valentine tank. This is the Mark VIII which carried a 6-pdr gun. The turret, although redesigned, was still very cramped even for a crew of two. Fitted to the side of the turret are a pair of 4-in smoke-bomb dischargers which could be fired from inside, providing the tank with cover in an emergency. Note also how the headlamps have been reversed on their mountings to avoid damage.

Moving a 6-pdr anti-tank gun into position behind a Jeep. This was hardly the usual means of hauling it since the gun weighed over a ton and there was no room on the vehicle for the crew, let alone ammunition. However, if a gun needed moving in a hurry to some difficult location a Jeep could just about cope.

Rommel made extensive use of mines at Mareth and many of these had to be cleared before any attack could be mounted. This poor but unusual photograph shows a Valentine fitted with the anti-mine roller attachment which appears to have come to grief. Most of the rolls have gone and the tank itself appears to have run over a mine just to complete the destruction.

Scorpion flails were used again at Mareth and proved far more effective at dealing with the mines. They had not been particularly successful at El Alamein but modifications to the design and improved operating techniques, in addition to increased experience on the part of the crews, made a lot of difference. Here a Matilda Scorpion gets in a bit of practice before the battle.

A wrecked Valentine of A Squadron, 50th RTR, lies abandoned in the flooded Wadi Zigzaou. The churned-up mess to its right could be the remains of one of the fascine causeways and, looking at the far bank, one wonders how the tanks were expected to deal with such a difficult climb in the face of enemy fire. A tank, rearing up over an obstacle of this sort, presents its vulnerable underside to waiting anti-tank guns long before it can bring its own gun to bear in reply.

Hood, a Headquarters Squadron tank of 50th RTR, was knocked out during the Mareth battle. The photograph was taken some years after the war when a party from the RTR, based in Libya, visited the site and examined many of the wrecks which, by that time, had been stripped by the locals and rusted by the weather.

The grave where Lieutenant M.C. Bodley of the Royal Scots Greys was laid to rest alongside his Stuart reconnaissance tank *Astra III*. Many Stuarts were converted to a reconnaissance role by removing their turrets, which reduced the silhouette and improved the performance by cutting down the weight. A pintle-mounted .30 Browning machine-gun has been fitted to the turret ring and the tank carries the diamond device of headquarters squadron. Bodley's grave has been neatly decorated with small-arms ammunition.

A pair of Panzer IV Specials knocked out on a Tunisian road. The circumstances are not recorded but the way their guns are pointing, to left and right, suggests that they were trying to run through an ambush. The tank in the foreground, being examined by the British soldier, has three kill rings painted on the gun barrel, just behind the muzzle brake.

An Eighth Army Sherman, decorated in typical style with enough equipment to stock a shop, rolls past abandoned German slit trenches on the road into Tunisia. The contrast of this fertile land to the barren desert to which these men were accustomed must have come as a pleasant change although it required much greater driving discipline.

Watched by Allied soldiers and a group of locals, an Eighth Army Sherman roars through the Gabes Gap. The bulldozer in the background has undoubtedly been employed to create the new roadway. It appears to have been fitted with improvised armour around the driver's seat which suggests that the spot was still vulnerable to enemy fire when the machine started work. Back down the road, transport can be seen moving in both directions.

British troops examine one of their most feared opponents, an 88-mm anti-aircraft gun, with the kind of fascination some people have for deadly snakes. There is plenty of evidence lying around in the form of spent shell cases to indicate a hard fight, but the unused ammunition, stacked on the right, proves that the gun was captured while it was still capable of fighting. It requires little imagination to picture how this must have looked at the height of the action.

Churchill tanks of First Army operating in the Tunisian hills. The leading tank is a Mark I which mounts a 2-pdr gun in the turret and a 3-in howitzer in the hull, to the left of the driver. Among the tanks in the background are some Mark III Churchills which had 6-pdr guns in a larger welded turret and a Besa machine-gun in the hull.

The Tiger tanks which led the attack at Hunts Gap came to a very sad end. Eight of them ran onto mines and seven more were either shot up by anti-tank guns or got themselves bogged down in the mud, leaving just four runners to get away. Two of the bogged tanks are shown here after a visit by the engineers who blew their turrets off, just to make sure they could not be recovered and used again.

Allied observers reported increasing appearances of self-propelled guns in action on the German side. One of the most common types was the SdKfz 139 or Marder III. It was an unusual combination: a Soviet 7.62-cm mounted on the chassis of a Czech-built Pzkw 38 light tank in Germany. Large numbers of these excellent guns had been captured on the Eastern Front and many of them were converted to fit self-propelled mounts. Sixty-six of these units were shipped to North Africa and this one is seen, after capture, towing a two-wheeled ammunition trailer.

British infantry, heavily armed with Bren guns, take cover at the roadside while a Universal Carrier shelters behind a Panzer IV Special. This combination suggests a rifle battalion which consisted of a headquarters company and four rifle companies. Each company comprised three Carrier Platoons, divided into four sections, each of which operated three Universal Carriers. The emphasis was on firepower, in the form of Bren light machine-guns and submachine-guns, with protected mobility provided by the Carriers.

Two Churchills about to cross a railway. Both are Mark III type with the 6-pdr gun. The climbing ability of these tanks, as demonstrated at Steamroller Farm, seems to have come as a surprise to their designers, as it did to the enemy. Indeed the tanks did not inspire much confidence when they first appeared and the failure rate resulted in an extensive rework programme organized by Vauxhall Motors. The Churchill had a complex, triple differential steering system which was responsible for many of the tank's problems but it also made it easier to manoeuvre up twisting mountain tracks.

British armoured car regiments were in constant demand and they spent much of the time split up, operating as independent squadrons, which was very popular with the young squadron commanders. These Daimler armoured cars of 11th Hussars were superb machines with an excellent cross-country performance and a 2-pdr gun which, in terms of firepower, placed them on a par with a Valentine tank. A rear-facing steering position enabled the Daimler to get itself quickly out of difficult situations.

An American-manned Jeep stands by while a half-track, armed with a 105-mm howitzer, bombards a distant target. Over 300 of these units were used in Tunisia but they were only ever regarded as a temporary measure pending the completion of more full-tracked, self-propelled guns. With a maximum range of 12,205 yd, firing a 33-lb shell, the 105-mm was an excellent weapon but it subjected the half-track's chassis to a good deal of punishment.

Many British commanders, especially those with desert experience, were critical of the Americans' approach to reconnaissance. They did not operate armoured cars, on the British or German pattern, and preferred to use light tanks such as these Stuarts. These were neither as small, fast nor quiet as armoured cars and this may well go some way towards explaining the cautious approach adopted by some American units. This is certainly why American commanders came to rely so heavily on the Derbyshire Yeomanry.

One of the most unpleasant weapons deployed by the Germans in Tunisia and elsewhere was the 15-cm Nebelwerfer multi-barreled mortar. Although described as a smoke mortar it could also launch a succession of six high-explosive rounds in about ninety seconds and there was nothing pleasant about being on the receiving end. Only a light vehicle was required to tow the weapon and it was easy to emplace but the crew was very vulnerable, as this picture shows.

One of the more unusual vehicles captured by the Americans in North Africa was this Saurer RR-7 armoured observation post. Built in Austria it operated on the obsolescent wheel-cum-track principle, meaning that it ran on wheels when it could, and tracks when it had to. It is shown here on tracks because the wheels have been removed, although the stub axles can still be seen. Changing from one mode to the other was mechanically controlled but in practice it was more trouble than it was worth.

Photographed under fire on a road near El Guettar a 75-mm Howitzer Motor Carriage T30 on a half-track chassis heads off at speed in the opposite direction. The gun in this case was the 75-mm M1 pack howitzer which was mounted behind a tall shield. Like most of these half-track mounted weapons it could only fire forwards. The gun had a maximum range of 9,610 yd, firing a 14-lb high-explosive shell, but as with others of this type the half-track variant was short-lived.

The scene at Wadi Akarit with Valentine tanks of 40th RTR gathering to be resupplied from their first line transport. Among the other vehicles visible here are tractors towing 6-pdr anti-tank guns and Universal Carriers. On the left can be seen a party of German prisoners being marched away.

Under the now silent gun of a knocked-out Panzer IV Special a 3-ton supply truck heads west. It carries the Sherwood Forest oak tree badge of British 46th (North Midland) Infantry Division. Having fought in France early in the war the division was now part of British First Army. The number 42 indicates the senior of three field regiments, Royal Artillery, while the sign above it identifies the battery. The turret marking on the German tank shows that this Panzer IV was the 2nd tank of the 5th platoon of the 8th company of its regiment.

CHAPTER 8
VICTORY IN TUNISIA

On 7 April 1943 a patrol from B Squadron, 12th Lancers met up with an American patrol from Benson Force. Representatives of Eisenhower's and Montgomery's armies shook hands. Having disengaged from the Wadi Akarit position the Germans made a disciplined retreat, under severe and constant air attack, with British forces close on their tail. The broad Tunisian coastal plain was no place to make a stand; every potential position could easily be outflanked and General Messe was inclined to head for Enfidaville at the northern end of the plain where the mountains again approached the coast. At first he was overruled but when the attack on Fondouk by 26th Armoured Brigade got underway it was finally agreed that this was the only place to go. Axis troops were in position at Enfidaville by 14 April.

From Enfidaville the Axis line ran due west and then slightly west of north to touch the coast again west of Bizerta. On average the line was about 40 miles from Tunis itself and, apart from the coastal plain in the east and the Medjerda river valley near the centre, it followed the high ground, some of which was incredibly rugged. Montgomery's Eighth Army, represented by 10th Corps, held the eastern end of the line, alongside the French Corps, part of First Army. Beyond them again were British 5th and 9th Corps with US II Corps holding the final section up to the coast. Naturally enough Montgomery wanted to take the initiative but he was told by General Alexander that the main thrust would be made in the centre. Alexander was anxious to get the fighting in North Africa over with swiftly and this meant preventing the Germans from retreating into the Cape Bon peninsula, east of Tunis, where they might be able to hold on for some time.

Thus Alexander's scheme was to take the most direct route to Tunis and split the Axis territory in two. The western half, including Bizerta, would be largely an American responsibility while British forces would sweep east, cut off Cape Bon and then head south down the coast, driving the enemy against the Eighth Army coming up from Enfidaville. The main attack was scheduled to begin on 22 April and, anticipating this, von Arnim did his best to spoil things by striking at assembly areas and forming up points. One such attack, by Tigers and Panzer IIIs of 504 Heavy Tank Battalion, was directed against the high ground of the Djebel Djaffa, where they established a strong defensive position. Here they were attacked by Churchill tanks of 48th RTR, in support of 40th Infantry Division. One of the German tanks knocked out in this action was Tiger 131, now displayed in the Tank Museum at Bovington. It was struck by two 57-mm rounds from a Churchill, one of which jammed the turret, causing the German crew to abandon the tank. It was the first Tiger captured intact by British troops and it was later inspected, in Tunis, by Prime Minister Winston Churchill and His Majesty King George VI.

An attack down the Mejerda valley first required that a major feature known as Longstop Hill be taken. It was the sort of position which the Germans believed to be impregnable. Infantry alone could not be expected to take it without sustaining terrible casualties and it was far too difficult for tanks to climb. However, that was to reckon without the Churchill and the regiment operating here, the North Irish Horse. Attacking on 26 April they scaled the heights of Longstop, providing close support for the infantry and causing the surviving Germans considerable surprise. It was the role of the Churchills at this time to break the crust of the enemy's defences with the infantry and, to use a popular phrase of the time, 'kick the door open' to enable the armoured divisions to roll through.

A few days before the Longstop battle the Churchills of 51st RTR, operating further east around Bou Arada, had attempted a similar incursion in order to clear a route for 6th Armoured Division but they encountered problems with mines that had not been cleared and, in the face of strong enemy fire, soon found that their infantry suffered heavy casualties. Those that survived, while prepared to go on, were too few in number and too exhausted to keep up with the tanks so, although some progress was made, it was not sufficient to enable the Shermans to push through.

The attack by the three regiments of 26th Armoured Brigade was made before dawn on 22 April, in an easterly direction and across a confused landscape of ridges and lakes. The operation was spearheaded by a regimental group comprising 16/5th Lancers, a battery of Priest self-propelled guns from 11th Regiment, Royal Horse Artillery, a Bofors anti-aircraft battery and A Company, 10th Rifle Brigade. They were followed by 17/21st Lancers and 2nd Lothian & Border Horse, similarly supported. There was much heavy fighting and all three regiments reported encounters with Tigers. The 16/5th told of one peculiar incident on 24 April. B Squadron, reporting itself low on ammunition, was ordered to withdraw while C Squadron made ready to replace it. The Germans mistook the move for a retreat and rushed in to occupy the area, only to run straight into C Squadron coming up. The enemy was chased off with considerable losses. Even so the defence was stubborn, and progress inevitably slow, so that on 27 April the tanks of 6th Armoured Division were withdrawn and those of 1st Armoured Division went in to support them.

Once this change had taken place the three original regiments rallied and then moved up again on the right. When they were all lined up the three regiments of 26th Armoured Brigade of 6th Armoured Division stood alongside the Bays, 9th Lancers and 10th Hussars of 2nd Armoured Brigade, 1st Armoured Division. It must have been quite a sight when they moved off, six armoured regiments more or less abreast, along with the Churchills of 51st RTR. Despite this preponderance of armour the attack stalled at the head of the valley which was covered by anti-tank guns controlled by observers on the ridges above. It is interesting to note that the three regiments of 1st Armoured Division, which, of course, had been transferred from Eighth Army, each still had one squadron of Crusaders to two of Shermans whereas the three regiments of 6th Armoured Division were fully equipped with Shermans. Another regiment mentioned at this time is the Yorkshire Dragoons, which appears to have been equipped with dummy tanks. It seems that in the days following the recent impasse a squadron of the Yorkshire Dragoons would move in to replace a regiment while it withdrew for a night's rest.

While the attack remained stalled 6th Armoured Division was pulled out on 26 April to refit at Bou Arada and on 3 May it moved down to join 7th Armoured Division near Medjez-el-Bab. The history of 17/21st Lancers mentions a large force of dummy tanks that replaced them at Bou Arada, presumably the Yorkshire Dragoons again. The new attack began on 6 May. The two armoured divisions were supported by four battalions of Churchills and some Scorpion mine-clearing flail tanks. The battle was inaugurated by a massive artillery bombardment and overwhelming air cover. Progress was not as rapid as General Alexander had hoped but it was good enough and many regiments noted a reduction in the intensity of opposition.

This was not so much a recognition of the inevitable as a near total breakdown of communications on the enemy side which meant that even senior commanders such as von Arnim were completely out of touch and forced to conduct local actions. A German report issued on 5 May declared that in the face of such a powerful attack the road to Tunis could not be held beyond 7 May. It proved quite correct. Armoured car patrols of 1st Derbyshire Yeomanry and 11th Hussars drove into the city on 8 May, a fitting result since these two highly professional regiments represented First and Eighth Armies respectively, and the 11th Hussars, in particular, had been in at the very start. The enemy took two escape routes. Some headed north-west for Cape Bon while the remainder withdrew towards Bizerta, no doubt reflecting upon the Führer's latest helpful order 'to resist to the last man'.

Meanwhile on the American front the fighting was just as hard. The 1st Armored Division followed the valley of the River Tine but encountered difficulties when they came up against enemy positions in the surrounding hills. The important road junction and river crossing at Mateur was taken on 3 May but now the US troops were faced with an added difficulty. Inland from Bizerta are two enormous lakes and it was necessary to split the force and move around both sides to secure the entire area. In fact units were spread out to cover as much ground as possible and four special task forces were sent forward from Mateur to envelop the eastern side of the lakes. All noted a lack of organization and reluctance to resist among the enemy troops and Bizerta, attacked from both sides, was entered by 894th Tank Destroyer Battalion at about the same time as British troops rolled into Tunis.

With Tunis in sight 6th Armoured Division was directed east to seal off the neck of the Cape Bon peninsular while 7th Armoured struck out north-west to meet the Americans at Protville. Meanwhile British 1st Armoured Division had been moving steadily across country towards Cape Bon. When 6th and 7th Armoured Divisions began their attack on 6 May the enemy tanks holding up 1st Armoured slipped away. Their advance as far as Creteville was relatively unopposed but they had to fight hard for the narrow pass that would take them through to Cape Bon. The situation was complicated by the fact that some units, like a large body from the Hermann Goering Division, were eager to

surrender while others continued to fight. Indeed it was an odd progress. At one moment they would be passing 88-mm guns, potent but abandoned by the roadside while at the next corner they might encounter similar guns still in action. They fought an inconclusive action with some enemy tanks on the evening of 8 May but the next day rolled into Grombalia where they met up with the Grenadier Guards.

On the previous day 6th Armoured Division had taken part in a most unusual action at a place called Hamman Lif, on the coast of the Gulf of Tunis. Heading south-east the regiment had come up against well-sited German guns at a spot where high ground ended in steep cliffs, virtually on the shore. For a while the tanks were held up while artillery and infantry attempted to dislodge the defenders overnight. This was reported as a successful operation but when the advance began next morning the German guns opened up again. With nowhere else to go the tanks, led by 2nd Lothian and Border Horse, raced along the beach and even into the sea, in order to smash their way through. The *Official History* claims that twenty-two Sherman tanks were lost in this bold action but the result was considered worth it.

With Cape Bon on their left the division reached the eastern coast at Hammamet and then turned south to press against the rear of General Messe's force, still holding up Eighth Army around Enfidaville. Meanwhile British 4th Infantry Division swept its way around Cape Bon. By now all units were reporting mass surrender.

White flags could be seen everywhere, except where ecstatic French residents showered the Allied troops with flowers and wine, sometimes even while fighting continued. The official surrender of all Axis forces in Tunisia was negotiated during the night 12/13 May and it came into effect shortly after midday on 13 May. General Alexander could report to Churchill, in London: 'We are masters of the North African shores.'

A Victory Parade, attended by the Prime Minister, was held in Tunis on 20 May and a few weeks later His Majesty King George VI came out to Tunisia and visited many of the regiments that had brought this dramatic conflict to a successful end.

Two officers of 12th Royal Lancers smile down at the photographer from the turret of their Humber armoured car. The regiment's role at this time was described as furnishing 'going reports' every two hours and protecting 22nd Armoured Brigade. Going reports, in military parlance, are descriptions of the terrain, signalled back to the tanks to prevent them from picking an unsuitable route.

A Valentine of 23rd Armoured Brigade passing through Ben Gardane, on the main highway about 100 miles west of Tripoli. The brigade at this time consisted of 40th RTR, strengthened by C Squadron, 50th RTR, amounting to forty-three Valentines in all. There was no fighting at Ben Gardane – the enemy had already gone – but it was slow going. Salt marshes prevented tanks from operating away from the road and the Germans had made sure, with mines and booby traps, that the road itself was not safe.

An American half-track, serving as a command vehicle, on patrol. The Americans seem to have picked up their style of stowage from the British Eighth Army; they certainly liked to travel well equipped. The racks along each side of the vehicle were designed to carry mines. British soldiers were very impressed by American communications equipment. Their main radio sets had powerful boosters which meant that they could function at long range. The short-range, hand-held 'walkie-talkie' sets were another novelty. One soldier studies a map board while the other sends in his report.

On the coastal plain any attempt to leave the road could result in a vehicle becoming bogged down in a salt marsh. This, at least, is what appears to have happened to this Panzer IV Special which has created a pair of deep furrows up to the point where it could go no further. It was at times like this that commanders had to resist the temptation to send another tank in to tow the first one out. The usual result was that both of them got stuck.

Eighth Army's pursuit of General Messe's troops to Enfidaville was a lively affair with everyone making the best possible speed. Here the plain appears to be covered with vehicles, mostly Universal Carriers and light trucks which suggests a rifle battalion. Although it all looks smooth and flat the ground close to the camera is quite rocky which could easily cause a Carrier to throw a track.

A pair of Panzer II light tanks knocked out and pushed to the side of the road. Both have lost their turrets and suffered other damage although by this stage in the war little tanks like this hardly represented a serious threat. By 1942 the surviving Panzer IIs had mostly been relegated to the reconnaissance companies of Panzer regiments. With a top speed of about 25 mph and a radius of action of around 100 miles they proved quite suitable for such work.

A sergeant major of 12th Lancers takes time off to sit in the sun and read a newspaper while his Daimler Dingo scout car appears to be charging up its battery from a local supply. A selection of old ammunition boxes is welded on to provide more stowage and this car, a Mark II, still retains the folding steel roof. This feature rapidly fell out of favour; if the Dingo ran over a mine when it was shut it increased the risk of injury to the crew.

Bishop self-propelled guns ready to fire on enemy positions in the Tunisian hills, May 1943. The Bishop was a Valentine tank which had its turret replaced by an armoured superstructure, containing a 25-pdr gun. Although arguably better than nothing, it was a poor design since it restricted the elevation of the gun and was cramped. Indeed one crew member is obliged to kneel outside, on the engine cover, which was both uncomfortable and dangerously exposed.

Posing for the camera a British soldier nonchalantly stares through his binoculars, uncomfortably close to a German Tiger tank. This one, however, is harmless, having been knocked out by 48th RTR at the Djebel Djaffa, on the road between Medjez-el-Bab and Montarnaud, 21 April 1943. The open hatches show that the Tiger's five-man crew baled out once their tank was hit. Some damage can be seen to the loader's hatch on the far side of the turret.

The Tiger, turret no. 131, proved to be something of a tourist attraction for British troops in the area until it was recovered. Nobody could fail to be impressed. The size of the Tiger was incredible enough but its thick armour and huge gun were bound to command respect. German trenches had been thrown up either side of the tank but their only occupant now is a British soldier. A Dingo scout car and Churchill tank thunder by in the background.

Considering that they were often created in a hurry some of the German defences in Tunisia were quite impressive. This is an anti-tank ditch located in front of the Axis position on Longstop Hill and it is quite deep and wide enough to stop any tank. It is also very long and must have taken considerable labour to excavate.

Churchill tanks of 142nd Regiment, Royal Armoured Corps (originally 7th Battalion the Suffolk Regiment), at the time of the Longstop Hill battle. Like some American vehicles these tanks have had mud pasted in an irregular pattern over the original green paint to break up their outline. The taking of Longstop cleared a key German position protecting the route to Tunis and it was the kind of work at which Churchill tanks excelled.

A diesel-powered M4A2 Sherman tank belonging to A Squadron of an unidentified British regiment in Tunisia. Despite the lack of markings the tank probably belongs to 7th Armoured Division which had been switched from Eighth Army to join First Army for the final drive on Tunis. The Shermans of 26th Armoured Brigade in 6th Armoured Division were painted green while this one is clearly of a lighter hue.

A knocked-out Panzer III with a dead crewman lying on the side. This is a late model, an Ausf. L armed with the long 5-cm gun. It has also had additional armour fitted to the front although this was not sufficient to dissuade the crew from adding more protection of their own in the shape of spare lengths of track. Not that this offered anything more than psychological protection but, since all tank crews did the same if they could, it was generally accepted by those in authority.

A Churchill Mark III of C Squadron, 51st RTR, and a Universal Carrier of 6th Armoured Division, as shown by the Mailed Fist badge on the left track guard. Notice how, on the Churchill, part of the offside track guard has gone. They were very vulnerable and it was actually more unusual to see a tank with them on if it had been in service for any length of time. With or without these guards the Churchill had an unpleasant habit of throwing up dust at the front which went straight into the driver's face.

British Shermans deploying on a plain. A complete brigade of three armoured regiments would field something in the region of 150 tanks and they must have been an impressive sight on the move. Although individually vulnerable to the larger German weapons these tanks would be unstoppable when used in mass formations. As long as the attacker was prepared to accept losses a proportion of the tanks would always get through, and with Shermans available in such quantities the result was almost inevitable.

Although ambivalent at first the French in Tunisia gradually came to see the Allies as liberators and most regiments record happy scenes involving the pleasant ingredients of flowers, girls and wine. Such celebrations even continued under fire. Here the crew of a 12th Lancers Dingo seem to be enjoying themselves in the latter stages of the race for Tunis.

On the American front the fighting was initially very hard. Here troops are occupying hill positions, supported by a 75-mm gun half-track M3. The gun in this case was an improved version of the celebrated French 75-mm from the First World War and in this vehicle it was used as a tank destroyer. A number of these units were later acquired by British armoured car regiments who used them to form a heavy troop providing, in effect, instant artillery support.

A pair of M10 tank destroyers of the US Army thunder past a Tunisian farm *en route* for Bizerta. Both vehicles have their turrets reversed so one cannot see the 3-in guns clearly. Based on Sherman chassis the M10s were not so well armoured and, as shown, had open top turrets. They were gradually replacing the 75-mm gun half-tracks in tank destroyer battalions at this time.

American troops in a captured German armoured car which they have covered with white stars just to be on the safe side. This is the SdKfz 233, an eight-wheel drive vehicle powered by a Bussing-NAG engine, carrying a short 75-mm Stuk37 gun in an open-top mounting. These big cars were designed to provide close support for armoured car units and they had an excellent cross-country performance. According to the original caption it was captured by American IInd Corps from 10th Panzer Division.

British troops examine the ammunition from a captured 88-mm gun. The rounds have been taken from a locker in the back of the gun tractor, a heavy three-quarter-track vehicle which also has seats for the entire gun detachment. Bearing in mind the size of the gun and its tractor it is quite remarkable that the Germans seemed capable of moving and emplacing them so easily. Most Allied tank crews were quite prepared to believe that there was an 'eighty-eight' around every corner, and quite often there was.

Grenadier Guards with their Universal Carriers moving into action. Notice the total absence of steel helmets. The 3rd Battalion was involved in the Kasserine Pass battle and subsequently operated with 6th Armoured Division, but once they had broken through towards Tunis the Guards, to quote their history, 'follow up three or four miles behind the tanks . . . and wait until the tanks found that they could make no further progress without the assistance of infantry'.

A Daimler armoured car leads a mixed column of armoured vehicles warily into Tunis. The second vehicle is an American-built White Scout Car, more like an armoured truck than its British counterpart, the Dingo. Most British regiments used Whites to carry essential items such as mine detectors and other stores which could not be fitted easily into armoured cars. The column includes Jeeps and Humber armoured cars.

Three Daimler armoured cars of 11th Hussars, photographed at an airfield outside Tunis. They have all been smartened up for the forthcoming victory parade with pennants flying and the crews in smart uniforms. The men sitting on the mudguards are in fact the drivers who would not otherwise have been seen in the picture!

Troops, Universal Carriers and Sherman tanks line the route in Tunis on 20 May 1943 as the Prime Minister, in a Humber staff car, leads the parade of senior officers to inspect the turn out. Interestingly, the vehicle behind Churchill's Humber is German, a Horch 40. One wonders if the fact that Rommel often used just such a car was appreciated by any of those involved?

His Majesty King George VI inspects the captured Tiger tank from the Djebel Djaffa action in Tunis. He is crouching by the open driver's hatch. The tank had been marked for the occasion with the black diablo device of 25th Tank Brigade and the shield of First Army. It was shipped back to Britain for a thorough technical evaluation later that year and is now one of the most popular exhibits in the Tank Museum at Bovington.

INDEX